HECTOR BERLIOZ

Books by Victor Seroff

DIMITRI SHOSTAKOVICH
The Life and Background of a Soviet Composer

THE MIGHTY FIVE
*(Balakirev, Borodin, Cui, Mussorgsky
and Rimsky-Korsakoff)*

RACHMANINOFF

MAURICE RAVEL

DEBUSSY, MUSICIAN OF FRANCE

RENATA TEBALDI
The woman and the diva / An intimate portrait

FREDERIC CHOPIN

WOLFGANG AMADEUS MOZART

FRANZ LISZT

HECTOR BERLIOZ

Opera Librettos in English

THE LOVE FOR THREE ORANGES
by S. Prokofiev

PRINCE IGOR
by A. Borodin

Hector Berlioz

BY VICTOR SEROFF

THE MACMILLAN COMPANY
New York

Quotations from Memoirs of Hector Berlioz *by Ernest Newman*
are reprinted with permission of the publisher. Copyright,
1932 by Alfred A. Knopf, Inc. Renewed, 1960 by Vera Newman.

The Macmillan Company, New York
Collier-Macmillan Canada, Ltd., Toronto, Ontario

Library of Congress catalog card number: 67–21253

Printed in the United States of America
First printing

PICTURE CREDITS: Barzun, Jacques, *Berlioz and the Romantic Century* (1950), 14, 156; Boschot, Adolphe, *Une Vie Romantique: Hector Berlioz* (1927), 47, 86; Culver Pictures, Inc., frontispiece (Portrait of Hector Berlioz by P. Sieffert), 5, 33 (bottom), 53, 139; Historical Pictures Service–Chicago, 6, 19, 39, 46, 59, 87, 96, 99, 107, 119, 142–143; Hopkinson, Cecil, *Bibliography of Musical and Literary Works of Hector Berlioz, 1803–1869* (1951), 134; Jullien, Adolphe, *Hector Berlioz: sa vie et ses oeuvres* (1888), 81, 108, 114, 159; Kapp, Julius, *Berlioz: eine Biographie* (1917), 91, 94; *Monde Musical* for Nov. 30, 1903, 152; Music Collection, New York Public Library, 29, 79; Picture Collection, New York Public Library, 30–31, 45, 62, 102, 130; Radio Times Hulton Picture Library, 8–9, 17, 23, 28, 33 (top), 36, 48, 60–61, 71, 76, 82, 103, 110–111, 124, 149. Picture research by Sally Raymond.

for Nelda Audibert,
in honor of a
long and true friendship

"Love can give no idea of music;
Music can give an idea of love.
Why separate them? They are
the two wings of the soul."

Hector Berlioz

Part One

Chapter One

"*I* came into the world quite naturally, unheralded by any of the signs which, in poetic ages, preceded the advent of remarkable personages," Hector Berlioz wrote at the age of forty-five in his *Mémoires*.

It was a modest but ironical statement from Berlioz, who at forty-five could already look back on a remarkable—and heralded—career.

Actually, in the world at large there was no scarcity of events when Berlioz was born on December 11, 1803, at the beginning of the nineteenth century. And in all that was taking place, France, Berlioz's native country, was a particular influence. While the European nations were still digesting the ideas brought about by the French Revolution, Napoleon was making preparations for further conquests with a plan to invade England, and delegates of President Jefferson, on behalf of the United States Government, were in Paris concluding the purchase of Louisiana.

Berlioz, born into these politically troubled times, would gain his laurels in an entirely different field—as a great musician who not only contributed to the development of Romantic music but through his compositions enhanced the sound of the symphonic orchestra to a level unsurpassed even in our time.

Strangely, perhaps, Berlioz was not born to a family of musicians. In fact at that time there was not a single piano in the small town of La Côte-Saint-André, his birthplace, some thirty-five miles northwest of Grenoble. And to make things even more difficult for the future composer, Berlioz's parents were very much against his choice of a musical profession.

While his father eventually acquiesced, his mother remained adamant, for in those days, in the minds of Frenchmen, musical and theatrical professions led to discredit in this world and damnation in the next. Was Hector, the eldest of their six children, to be the first to challenge the respected standards of his forebears, to whom music was merely a means of diversion?

The long list of these Berlioz ancestors can be traced to the beginning of the seventeenth century. Some of them were connected with the local tanning industry, others were men of wealth and education; but not a single musician among them. Most of them had lived at La Côte-Saint-André, where Hector's grandfather, a lawyer by profession, rebuilt the family's large stone house. The house, as Hector's birthplace, was made into a museum in 1935.

Hector's father, Louis Berlioz, had given up his studies of law in favor of medicine and became a well-respected physician, especially after his essay on "Chronic Diseases" won the prize offered by the medical society of Montpellier in 1810. In addition to medicine, which he practiced more as a means for doing good for his fellowmen than for gaining wealth, Dr. Berlioz was greatly interested in literature and philosophy and had learned English and Italian. According to Hector, his

*The birth-
place of
Hector
Berlioz in
La Côte-
Saint-André*

father was a freethinker, "that is to say, he had no prejudices, social, political, or religious," but he had promised Hector's mother to do nothing to unsettle the faith which she regarded as indispensable to Hector's salvation.

Hector's mother, Maria Antoinette Josephine, born Marmion, was twenty-one, five years younger than her husband, when they were married in 1802. Tall and good-looking, the daughter of a Grenoble lawyer, she found little opportunity at La Côte-Saint-André to use her social gifts, and the suppression of her abundant energy developed in her both a hypochondria and a devotion to religion. Maria's influence in raising Hector as a member of the Roman Catholic Church lost its power as he grew up, however. And yet while she hoped through religion to guard him from his "musical inclinations," it was in the church that Hector, for the first time, was deeply moved by music.

At the age of twelve and a half he was taken for his First Communion to the Convent of the Ursulines, where his sister Nanci, three years younger than he, was being educated. Although he was impressed by the ceremony, it was the eucha-

Louis Berlioz

ristic hymn sung by the chorus—as he went up to the altar to receive the sacrament—that overwhelmed him. The music, he said much later, revealed to him a world more glorious than the heaven of which he had heard so much.

The impression was so strong that even years later he distinctly remembered the rare atmosphere of that bright, fragrant spring morning, his kneeling among the white-robed young girls, and the priest's intonation of the solemn service. Nor was the memory of this first musical experience later marred by his discovery that the motet which had been introduced into the ceremony was adapted from Nicolas Dalayrac's opera *Nina, or The Woman Crazed with Love*. Sacred words had been put to the original aria, *"Quand le bien-aimé reviendra!"* ("When the beloved returns!")

At about that time Hector also learned something of Haydn and of the quartets by Ignaz Joseph Pleyel, thanks to the amateur violinists who, after Sunday mass, used to take pleasure in playing secular music at the Berlioz home. But though he was already drawn to music, until he was twelve there had been no one who was interested in teaching him to play an instrument, and therefore he played none—except for the drum, which he had learned at the school where he was sent at the age of six.

This school was one of many all over France devoted to raising, through military discipline, the young generation in absolute faith in and devotion to Napoleon, their Emperor. But Hector had been there only two years when the school was closed and he had to return home, where his father took complete charge of his education.

That Hector's childhood and adolescence were spent at home had a definite effect on his character. He was denied the normal companionship of schoolmates, of sharing their interests and taking part in their games, and thus he was much alone, for he was not really congenial with his sister Nanci. His favorite of the family was Adèle, born a year before his second sister, Louise, died at the age of eight in 1815. But Adèle was eleven years younger than Hector, and their close friendship did not develop until much later, when he was twenty-five.

On the subject of a home education, Berlioz later observed that it has fewer advantages than that of a public school; that, as in his own case, children are thrown almost exclusively into a relationship with their elders, a relationship which in the French middle class always remains formal, leaving the children unaware of the world and the realities of life. "I know perfectly well that at twenty-five," Berlioz recalled, "I was still an awkward, ignorant child"—ignorant of human behavior outside of his family, perhaps, but otherwise Hector was far from being an ignorant boy.

Under his father's tutelage he studied Latin, history, mathematics, French literature, geography, and even astronomy, and on his own he was an avid reader of travel and adventure tales, which he found in his father's library. However, one should not imagine that he spent his growing years glued to a desk. Hector was no hothouse plant; he had a fairly robust constitution and was a passionate mountain climber, a pastime which evoked in him an appreciation of the beauties of nature unusual in a boy of his age.

La Côte-Saint-André, as its name indicates, is a ridge stretching eight hundred feet east and west over the Rhone valley. From the small hillside town of the same name one looks over a vast panorama of fertile plains framed by a chain of mountains, behind which rise the snowcapped peaks of the Alps. The landscape of the surrounding countryside, its valleys intersected by rivers and mountain torrents, its constantly changing weather, temperature and light, and its majestic silence, all became important factors in Hector's imagination. It was natural that the boy should be a dreamer.

But his sheltered life did not prevent Hector from experiencing, as he recalled later, the pangs of that great passion described with so much power by Virgil, whose works in Latin he was assiduously studying under his father's guidance. It was his "first love," but so strong was it that "no after-loves

The Grenoble countryside in the early nineteenth century

could blot out the first," he remarked later in his *Mémoires*.

The object of the twelve-year-old boy's infatuation was the tall, slender Mademoiselle Estelle Duboeuf. She was eighteen. It was not her large expressive eyes or her mass of hair (which in his memory—although he later forgot the color—might have waved on the casque of Achilles), but her pink shoes which struck the fatal blow to his heart. Hector had never before seen a pair of pink shoes.

It was almost traditional that for three weeks at the end of each summer Hector's mother, taking along her children, would visit her father at his country home in Meylan, three miles from Grenoble. The home had a splendid view of the most beautiful landscape Hector had ever seen. It included a small white villa surrounded by gardens and vineyards, against the background of the massive Saint Eynard rock and an ancient ruined tower. In this villa, during the summer months, Estelle stayed with her grandmother. It was a perfect setting for romance.

As further incitement, his heroine's name was associated in Hector's mind with *Estelle*, a pastoral novelette by the French poet Jean Pierre Claris de Florian (1755–1794). Hector had discovered the book in his father's library and, as he said, was "devouring" it in secret. Written with artificial delicacy and extreme sentimentality, the long-drawn-out story deals with the romance of Estelle, a shepherdess, and Némorin, a shepherd, describing in detail the sufferings caused them by Estelle's father, who felt it was his moral duty to have his daughter marry the son of a friend who had once saved his life.

Primarily a poet, Florian managed to incorporate into the six chapters (some one hundred and fifty pages) not less than twenty-one poems, full of virtue and moral axioms, which appealed to Hector as much as the subject of the story.

The boy's relatives, cousins, uncles, and aunts often gathered at his grandfather's home, and the fateful meeting of Hector with Estelle took place one evening at a large outdoor party when the guests were playing a game called "prisoner's base." The young men and women were to be divided into two teams, the men choosing their female partners. As if everyone sensed Hector's fast-beating heart, he was called upon to make his choice first. Blushing, his eyes fixed on the ground where Estelle stood, he remained motionless: he dared not utter the name of his chosen partner.

"Well then, I will choose—I take Monsieur Hector," Estelle announced, taking him by the hand. Hector was more hurt than happy, for he did not miss the flirtatious glance that Estelle threw at his uncle, Felix Marmion, a young cavalry officer.

Uncle Felix was everything that could dazzle an eighteen-year-old girl. In addition to his resplendent captain's uniform, he bore two marks of the military campaigns in which he had participated: a bullet wound in his left foot and a saber-scar across his cheek, mere trifles as far as he was concerned, for in his devotion to Napoleon he would have given his life. Felix often regaled the company with first-hand accounts of the Emperor and also played the violin and sang popular songs well enough to win the admiration of the young ladies. No wonder Hector suffered from jealousy, love's ghostly companion, and even years later shuddered when he recalled the ring of his rival's spurs as Felix danced with Estelle.

Thereafter hopelessly in love, Hector withdrew into himself more and more, evoking in his imagination every detail of his beloved's image, her every pose and gesture, and repeating to himself the few words she happened to address to him whenever he saw her at his grandfather's home or at picnics in the mountains, which now he never missed. Nursing his desperate feelings, he would often hide himself in the cornfields and spend nights in sleepless anguish.

During the following seventeen years he did not see Estelle. He heard that she had married, but he did not know her married name or where she lived. It was of no importance to him, it did not affect his feelings—he was still in love with her. Hector was nearly thirty years old when, during a visit home, his mother asked him to deliver a letter to a certain woman passing through their town. "Go to the coach station and, while they are changing horses, ask for Madame Fornier." Hector was unaware of the cruel trick his mother was playing on him.

He walked up to the door of the stagecoach and asked for Madame Fornier. "It is I," he heard the woman say as she took the letter; and then the coach drove off. Hector recognized the "dear voice," the hair, the smile. But did she recognize *him*? Probably not, he thought. And like a wounded bird he returned home. "Ah, I see," his mother teased him. "Némorin has not forgotten his Estelle!" Indeed Hector Berlioz never forgot *his* Estelle.

Chapter Two

As his twelfth year marked the beginning of his emotional life, it can also be considered the beginning of Hector Berlioz's musical activities. Two years previously he had found a flageolet (whistle-flute) in a drawer, and he tried so long to pick out some popular tunes on it that his father, to prevent his continual false "tooting," finally taught him to play the instrument, as well as to read music.

Hector showed such aptitude that his father saw no harm in letting the boy learn to play the flute under the tutelage of a Monsieur Imbert, whom Louis Berlioz, together with a few other music amateurs at La Côte-Saint-André, had imported from Lyons. Having been promised a few pupils and a fixed salary as conductor of the military band of the Garde Nationale, Imbert willingly abandoned his position as a second violinist in the orchestra of the Théâtre des Célestins in Lyons. Hector had two lessons a day and, as he also had a pleasant alto voice with which to make music, he soon became a good sight reader. In addition to the flageolet and flute, Hector later learned to play the guitar under Monsieur Dorant, who replaced Imbert.

These instruments and the drum were the only ones Hector Berlioz ever learned to play. To have let him study the piano, even if one could have been obtained for him, Louis Berlioz realized, would have furthered Hector's interest in music perhaps to the point of a devotion, which might have given him the idea of becoming a musician—and that certainly was against his parents' plans for their son's future.

Hector himself did not miss playing the piano. From the beginning of his interest in music he never had any inclination to become a performing instrumentalist. His sole desire was to compose. Later, speaking as a composer, he did say that playing the piano could have been of great value to him, but he added on second thought that considering the "appalling number of miserable musical platitudes to which the piano had given birth, and which would have never seen the light of day had their authors been confined to pen and paper," he felt grateful to the happy chance which forced him to compose freely, without having to keep in mind the technical complexities of a particular instrument.

Like so many other composers, Berlioz was self-taught. Using already existing compositions as examples, he experimented as best he could, inadequately more often than successfully. Gradually he gained sufficient experience to complete some chamber works, including a quintet for flute and strings, which he performed with some of the visiting musicians in his home, and also a sextet. The general tone of his compositions was melancholic, reflecting his unhappy love affair, and as he was still rereading Florian's *Estelle* and identifying himself with Némorin, he took several verses from the book and set them to music.

Among these settings one was particularly doleful, for the verse seemed to have expressed his despair at leaving the woods and the spots which had been "honored by her steps, illuminated by her eyes," and, as Berlioz later added, "by the pink shoes of my cruel fair one." It is not surprising that as a mature composer Berlioz regarded both the verse and his own interpretation as insipid rather than romantic, as it had seemed to him at the time. Yet although he destroyed these compositions, years later he was happy to remember one of the melodies, and he used it when he began to write his *Symphonie fantastique* (in 1829).

His youthful compositions, however, were no justification to his father of Hector's desire to devote himself entirely to music. Fascinated by the romantic, artistic lives of Haydn and Gluck, whose biographies he had read, Hector pleaded in vain with Louis Berlioz, who was determined to have him become a physician like himself. Louis went so far as to bribe his son by promising him the latest model flute, "with all the new keys," if Hector agreed to work at osteology.

For a boy whose thoughts were of poetry and music it was boring to sink into a large volume of Monro's treatise, with its life-size illustrations of the structure of the human body.

*Hector Berlioz
in his youth*

Fortunately he was joined in these studies by his cousin Alphonse Robert, who played violin well enough to take part in Hector's quartets. Alphonse was very serious about his studies and eventually became a prominent physician. Although Hector preferred discussing music, under his cousin's influence he progressed sufficiently to go to the medical school in Paris.

As a requirement for admission he passed the examinations for a bachelor's degree at Grenoble, and later that year, during the winter of 1821, the two young men went to Paris. But one would be underestimating Hector's sincere devotion to music if one imagined him abandoning his dreams of a musical profession—the only profession, in his opinion, for which he was suited. While trying to widen his musical education on the side, however, he did keep his promise to his father and pursued his medical studies.

On his father's rather generous allowance of one hundred and twenty francs a month, and sharing lodgings with Alphonse in the Rue Saint Jacques on the Left Bank, Hector could live quite well as a student. Now almost eighteen, he was an attractive youth with deep-set blue eyes and a prominent high-bridged nose, his head crowned with a mass of fiery red-blond hair falling over his broad forehead. He was five feet three in height and broad-shouldered. His expressive features no longer betrayed his melancholia but showed curiosity and at times enthusiasm as he reacted to the new impressions of the capital.

However, though he was still a provincial lad—an awkward youth, as he himself admitted later—he was more disappointed than impressed by the social life to which he was introduced through the Berlioz family friends in Paris and through his Uncle Felix, who was often in the capital on leave from his regiment. Hector decided that the amusements of Paris society differed from those he had been used to at home merely

in the number of guests—sixty instead of sixteen—and in the
fact that evening dress was obligatory and that they danced
on a crowded floor to the accompaniment of two violins and
a flageolet—a pitiful ensemble at best—whose repertory con-
sisted of *contredanses* taken from the ballets of well-known
operas.

He seemed almost to prefer the bohemian life of the Latin
Quarter, among his fellow students in medicine, where he was
at least spared the amateur's empty talk of art. But this pleas-
ant life was marred almost at his first contact with the medical
school. It was not Gay-Lussac's lectures on experimental elec-
tricity, or Professor Amussat's teaching of anatomy (the latter
with an artistic passion that reminded Hector of his own love
for music), but the practical side of medical studies that
shocked him.

It was one thing to study anatomy following the illustrations
on his desk in the pleasant surroundings of his home at La
Côte-Saint-André, but quite another thing when Alphonse
took him to the dissecting room at the Hôpital de la Pitié.
Hector almost fainted when they entered the place with its
litter of corpse fragments, its ghastly faces and open skulls, the
sparrows fighting over bits of lungs, rats gnawing at bleeding
vertebrae, and the suffocating stench.

It took all Alphonse's eloquence to persuade Hector against
immediately giving up his career as a physician. Hector never
had wholeheartedly agreed either with his father or with Al-
phonse that the medical profession was the finest in the world,
and he certainly hated the thought of spending his life at the
bedside of the sick and in hospitals, but he nevertheless con-
sented to continue his studies, as otherwise he would have
jeopardized his stay in Paris where so much music was avail-
able to him.

A street in the Paris student quarter in the 1800's

For the first time in his life he heard an opera, and "the gorgeous splendor of the spectacle, the rich fullness of the orchestra and the chorus," overwhelmed him. This experience made him feel much like a boy who, although he has the in-born instincts of a sailor, has never seen anything but fishing boats on a lake and then is suddenly transported to an ocean liner. Hector attended several more performances with con-stantly growing enthusiasm and, after he saw Gluck's *Iphi-génie en Tauride,* he vowed to become a musician, come what may, even against his parents' and his friends' advice to give up the pursuit of a chimera.

But true to his promise to his father, two years later (Janu-ary, 1824) Hector did become a Bachelor of Sciences, an accomplishment managed "on the side," as he was wholly absorbed in his musical studies all the while.

At the Paris Conservatory library, where he was working as best he could over the opera scores, Hector often met with another student of music named Gerono. Gerono suggested Hector try to join the composition class under Jean François Lesueur which he attended. Eventually Hector summoned his courage and called on the esteemed professor, bringing with him his cantata and a canon for three voices, which he felt were appropriate to the solemn occasion.

Lesueur looked through the scores, impressed by some ele-ments of dramatic feeling but noting also that they showed Hector's complete ignorance of harmony and composition. Lesueur advised Hector to take some lessons from Gerono before he would accept him in his class. It was the first rec-ognition and encouragement Hector had received, and he worked so hard that a year later (1823) he became Lesueur's pupil, and eventually his favorite.

He enjoyed his teacher's friendship to the last days of the master's life, although when no longer his pupil Hector was rather critical of Lesueur's theories of composition. "What

Jean François Lesueur

precious hours I wasted," he remarked, "first, in studying his antediluvian theories, then in practicing them, and finally in unlearning them."

But Berlioz was by no means ungrateful to Lesueur. As his mentor, he had given him a fundamental knowledge of composition when Hector had none, as well as having introduced him to the general meaning and purpose of music. As the composer of a large number of masses, Lesueur ignited Hector's interest in the stories of the Old Testament and in the legends of the East; and as a man, confiding to Hector his own biography, Lesueur acquainted the youth with another side of the romantic life of an illustrious musician.

He told him of the petty enmities of fellow composers, of the difficulties he had had in getting his first opera produced, of the anxieties on the night of its first performance, and of the lassitude which followed. These reminiscences made their walks along the Seine, and the long afternoons spent in the Tuileries gardens, unforgettable. For years afterward Berlioz could remember the sight of his old master, after they had parted, slowly going home through the shady allées of the garden, silent in his reveries.

After only a few months of studying with Lesueur, Hector decided to write an opera. For this bold attempt he needed a libretto. Having heard from Lesueur of the difficulties in getting an opera accepted for production, Hector addressed himself to François Guillaume Andrieux, whose courses in literature he had been attending and whose influence with the jury at the Opéra, so Hector believed, would be of paramount value to his venture.

Wishing him every success with his project Andrieux said in reply:

"The work you propose is not for a man of my age; my ideas and studies all lie in another field, and you would consider me a savage if I told you how long it has been since I have set foot in the opera house. I am sixty-four, and it would ill become me to write love poems; and as for the music, these days I should only be thinking of requiems. If you had only come to me thirty or forty years earlier, we could have worked together."

Thereupon, Hector asked his friend Gerono, who dabbled in poetry, to dramatize Florian's *Estelle*. Apparently the young lady with the pink shoes was still the natural heroine of his romance. It was fortunate, Berlioz later remarked, that no one ever heard a note of this composition, for his score was just as feeble as Gerono's poem.

Undaunted by his failure, Hector composed a series of scenes based on Bertrand Saurin's *Beverley, ou le Joueur*, a melodrama which he felt genuinely portrayed modern life. The composition was for bass voice with orchestral accompaniment, and Hector had no difficulty in imagining a success for it—if the bass were Dérivis and the orchestra that of the Théâtre Français. He even found the appropriate occasion for his project—the benefit performance for François Joseph Talma, the great tragedian. All Hector needed was Talma's consent to put his composition on the program. But bold as he was in his project, his courage failed him as he stood at the door of Talma's house. Twice he raised his hand to ring the bell, and twice he let it fall.

Soon afterward, however, Hector was comforted by a request to write a mass for All Innocents' Day (December 26) 1823, for performance at the Church of Saint Roch. He chose "The Crossing of the Red Sea" as his subject and, although Lesueur approved the score, which Berlioz later said was a poor copy of Lesueur's own style, the work did not get further along than the first rehearsal. But this time it was not Hector's fault.

Monsieur Masson, the conductor at the Church of Saint Roch, had promised Hector a hundred picked musicians in the orchestra, a still larger chorus, and a month for rehearsing the work. But on the day of the first full rehearsal the instrumental and choral forces dwindled to twenty singers and twelve children in the chorus and in the orchestra nine violins, one viola, an oboe, a horn, and a bassoon. Hector was in despair. But Masson assured him that everybody would appear for the performance on the morrow, and he insisted on going through with the rehearsal.

Then came the *coup de grâce* that put an end to the conductor's endeavor. It became apparent that the orchestral and vocal parts, copied gratis by the Saint Roch choir children, were so full of mistakes that it was impossible to proceed with the performance.

It was a cruel introduction to the complexities of managing a large body of performers, and a cruel way of dashing Hector's hopes of impressing his parents and thus winning them over to his still-debated choice of profession. But the lesson was not lost. Having discovered the principal defects in his composition, he almost immediately began rewriting the whole score. He also realized that he had paid dearly for the "gratis" copying of the score's parts by the inexperienced young choristers. Since he could not afford to pay anybody else to do it, Hector undertook this task himself and finished within three months.

But after all the work was done and the score was in a presentable state he was still faced with the purely financial dilemma of getting it performed. He had been promised the use of the Opéra orchestra but at his own expense and, as for the singers he had in mind, he did not know them personally and could not ask for favors. The endeavor needed a large sum of money, which Hector did not have.

Remembering how his shyness had lost him the chance of getting a scene from his *Beverley, ou le Joueur* on Talma's program, Hector this time took a bold step by writing to the popular poet-statesman François René Chateaubriand for financial help and an introduction to the powers that be. Chateaubriand's reaction, clearly and cordially expressed in a reply sent from his country estate, was as might have been expected.

"You ask me for twelve hundred francs," Chateaubriand wrote. "Sir, I would send them to you if I had them. I cannot assist you as regards the ministry. I sympathize most truly with your difficulties. I love art, and honor artists, but talent often owes its triumphs to its trials; and the day of success compensates for all that one has suffered. Please accept all my regrets; they are very real."

Chateaubriand's pompous sermon did not assuage Hector's discouragement, particularly since, during his first summer at home after two years in Paris, he was confronted again with his old argument with his father.

But upon his return to Paris he was fortunate enough to meet, at the Opéra, Augustin de Pons, who had witnessed the fiasco of Hector's *Mass* during its first rehearsal. De Pons, a man of independent means and a great amateur of music, now

The Church of Saint Roch in Paris

inquired about the fate of this *Mass*. On hearing of Hector's predicament, he immediately offered him assistance.

Hector lost no time in assembling his chosen "musical forces," and on July 10, 1825, at the Church of Saint Roch the *Mass* was given its first performance. It was a success with the audience and the critics, and—what Hector valued most— it pleased Lesueur, who said to him: "You should not be a doctor or druggist or anything else but a great musician."

Hector, however, was even more attentive now to every criticism of his work and, after its second performance two years later in the Church of Saint Eustache, he realized the inferiority of the composition. Preserving the *Resurrexit* section he destroyed the rest of the score, along with the score of his attempt at the opera *Estelle*.

He learned much from these first experiments in composing, as he did from his first appearance as a conductor, when he barely managed to plow through the second performance of the *Mass*. "How little I then possessed of the qualities necessary to a good conductor," Berlioz, one of the great conductors of his time, later remarked. "I lacked the precision, flexibility, passion, and sensitivity, as well as that indefinable subtle instinct. How much time, practice, and thought have I spent in acquiring even a few of these!"

Little did he know that his trials—though they were eventually to bear out his faith in himself—were now only just beginning.

To start with, the long-smoldering controversy with his parents had reached its inevitable crisis. When Louis Berlioz heard of Hector's trying to enter the Conservatory (although Lesueur's student, Hector was not officially enrolled), he threatened to cut off his allowance. Lesueur tried to help by writing to Dr. Berlioz and pleading Hector's cause. But he made a fatal mistake in invoking religious principles to give more weight to his arguments. "Sir, I am an unbeliever!" began Dr. Berlioz in a letter to Lesueur suggesting he should mind his own business. And as for Hector, he was ordered to return home.

The tense cold atmosphere at home plunged Hector into a deep gloom. Once again his father declared an ultimatum: Hector must choose another profession or he could not return to Paris. Days and weeks passed during which Hector barely spoke to anybody and shut himself in his room or wandered about the woods trying in vain to find some solution. At last one morning, his father stated his willingness to give him one final chance to pursue his ambition. He would let his son go back to Paris, but if he should fail this time, Hector would have to put aside once and for all his claim to a professional career in music.

His father's announcement was so unexpected that the jubilant Hector could not conceal his excitement. Dr. Berlioz, wishing to avoid unpleasant scenes with Hector's mother, had made Hector promise to keep his departure a secret until the time came. But Hector confided in Nanci, and Nanci kept the secret as well as Hector. Before long everybody in the family, as well as their friends, knew about it, and when the news reached Hector's mother she gave vent to one of her periodical tantrums.

She began by accusing her husband of weakness in encouraging Hector's "wicked" plans. Then, falling on her knees in front of her son, she humbly begged him to give up his venture. And finally, in her wrath, she renounced him as her son. "Go and wallow in the filth of Paris, sully our name, and kill your father and myself with sorrow and shame!" she cried, closing her tirade with: "I will not reenter the house until you have left it. You are no longer my son. I curse you!"

And Madame Berlioz kept her word. She fled to a nearby country house belonging to the Berlioz family. There, on the day of his departure, Hector, accompanied by his father and his sisters, came to bid her goodbye. She was sitting under a tree in the orchard, reading. As soon as she saw them, she ran away. In vain they called to her. Hector Berlioz had to start on his musical career with his mother's curse upon his head.

Chapter
Three

*I*t was not long before Hector's new agreement with his father was again disturbed. While visiting with the family prior to Hector's departure, his cousin Alphonse had inadvertently told Dr. Berlioz about Augustin de Pons having lent Hector the necessary sum for the first performance of his *Mass*. Fearing his father's wrath while his consent was so newly won, Hector minimized his debt to De Pons, saying it was four hundred instead of twelve hundred francs.

Hector claimed that he could save enough from his allowance to pay the debt. And indeed he tried. When he returned to Paris in the fall of 1826, he went to live in a cheap little room on the sixth floor of an old dilapidated house. Instead of taking his meals in restaurants he tried to appease his hunger by dining on dry bread and raisins or prunes, while enjoying the sunsets over the Seine. Meanwhile he had entered the Conservatory, where he was assigned to Anton Reicha's class of counterpoint and fugue, which, according to the Conservatory rules, had to precede Lesueur's class in composition. Thus Hector was working under two professors at the same time. In addition, he continued composing on his own, but after five months he had no extraordinary accomplishment to show his father.

Dr. Berlioz—and Hector was well aware of it—most probably expected to hear that his son's genius had won unprecedented acclaim and that he was producing with the abundant regularity of a geyser. Instead he received a letter from De Pons, who, prompted by financial necessity, asked him to pay the remaining sum of Hector's debt.

Dr. Berlioz sent the money to De Pons and a letter to Hector, informing him that his monthly allowance was being stopped. It was a humiliating blow, but it was not in Hector's nature to admit defeat, even in the face of inevitable destitution. His only recourse was private pupils, which he could not catch as easily as the mice in his room. Thanks to Lesueur he eventually obtained a few students of flute and guitar at a price of one franc per lesson—not enough to pay for a gentleman's breakfast.

But Hector could not rely on these "here today, and gone tomorrow" music amateurs, and he looked for a job at one of the theaters as a flutist in the orchestra or a singer in the chorus. At last he was lucky. He was engaged as a chorus singer at the Théâtre des Nouveautés, where vaudeville and a certain type of *opéra-comique* were performed. His salary was to be fifty francs a month—almost half of his former allowance. In addition to this sudden turn in his fortunes he met an old friend, Antoine Charbonnel, who had come to Paris to study chemistry and wanted to live in the Latin Quarter.

The two soon came to an expedient conclusion: since both had no money to speak of, they would join forces and pool what little they did have. They established bachelor quarters in two little furnished rooms in one of the less glamorous streets of the student district. Now that the winter was approaching Hector abandoned his "dining room" on one of the bridges across the Seine. His roommate was an expert cook and Hector profited by his example in the culinary art. On thirty francs a month each they lived "like two princes in exile."

In fact, for one hundred and ten francs Hector bought a piano, although he could not play a note. After all, he was convinced that he was a musician, and part of being a musician is owning a piano, if only as a piece of furniture. Although he never learned to play a single instrument except the flute, guitar and drums, Berlioz wrote in his *Mémoires:* "I like to have musical instruments in the room with me; and if I were rich, while I worked I would always have a concert grand piano, two or three Erard harps, and a collection of Stradivari violins and cellos."

Hector well knew that his parents would have been very chagrined to hear that he was working as a chorus singer in a theater—sure indication that he had taken the "wicked" path of his mother's dire predictions—and he kept secret even from his roommate the means by which he was earning his living. He regarded his job as merely temporary, for he was preparing

The Quai des Orfèvres on the Seine

Anton Reicha

himself to enter a competition for the Prix de Rome, as a way of solving his financial problems. The winner of the Prix was granted a scholarship for five years, three of which had to be spent in Italy.

Hector Berlioz's individual approach to music dates from the very beginning of his studies at the Conservatory. He respected Reicha, his teacher in counterpoint and fugue. but while willing to study the intricacies of fugue structure, he could not wholeheartedly agree with the indiscriminate use of fugues in compositions. When Hector asked Reicha why whole fugues were written on the single word "Amen" or on "Kyrie eleison," so frequent in masses and requiems, Reicha's sole explanation was "because everybody has done it and is still doing it."

This was no help to Hector, who thought that the constant repetition of the same words in different sections resembled nothing more than the incoherent shouts of a crowd of drunkards. He felt differently when the fugal form was applied as a means of expression—when it served to bring a subject to its glorious climax and was accompanied by words that justified the meaning of the whole composition.

Hector learned the art of orchestration not from Reicha, nor even Lesueur, but by carefully following the score of a work during an opera or concert performance. To acquaint himself with the sound and range of individual instruments, of which he had only scant knowledge, he asked his friends to experiment with him in different instrumental combinations. No wonder that the composition for full orchestra which he submitted to the Prix de Rome competition was judged by the jury as "unplayable."

As a subject, the competitors were given "The death of Orpheus at the hands of Bacchantes," for which they were to write a lyric scene or a brief cantata. The fairly competent pianist who played the works for the jury had no difficulty with the scores of all the other competitors since they were originally written at the keyboard. But Hector's was different, because it was conceived and written directly as an orchestral score, with no regard for the purely pianistic problems which were now baffling the jury's pianist.

The interior of the
Paris Opéra

It might have been considered "unplayable" at the time, yet it was the first of Hector's orchestral works to show his outstanding musical personality.

Whether because the unfavorable result of the competition overwhelmed him with "rage and despair," or because the hateful work in the chorus was such a constant strain on his nervous system, Hector now suffered an attack of quinsy. He was in agony for days until finally, to prevent "death from taking [his] young life," he lanced the abscess in the back of his throat. He used his old penknife.

Dr. Berlioz must have heard of his son's surgical exploit, for soon afterward he reinstated Hector's monthly allowance, which automatically put an end to his work in the chorus and left him free from immediate financial problems to pursue his musical studies. These were now centered on dramatic works.

For each performance he attended at the Opéra, Hector prepared himself by assiduously studying the score of the work he was to hear, and then, though he knew practically every note by heart, he would follow the performance with the score in his lap. Thus he acquired not only an intimate knowledge of composers' works but developed a taste and a preference for some that even bordered on bias. In discussion with his fellow students he would communicate his views and sharpen his evaluations. A whole group of these students, with Hector as their leader, would arrive at the Opéra long before curtain time to usurp the "best seats" in the orchestra pit, where students were allowed to sit free or for the price of a cheap ticket.

As if they were members of his orchestra, Hector supervised his friends' preparedness for the performance by supplying a libretto at the last moment or by pointing out in his score the significant passages they should not miss. Most of them, like Hector, favored Gluck above all other opera composers, and those who were still doubtful were quickly initiated into the cult of Gluck by Hector's authoritative comments, which he freely delivered during a performance.

The audience was disturbed less by this loud running commentary than when Hector would raise his voice in protest of some mishap which might occur on the stage or in the orchestra. "Hey, there are no cymbals there; who has dared to improve on Gluck?" Hector's powerful voice was heard to cry during a performance of *Iphigénie en Tauride*; and, on another occasion, "Not two flutes, you scoundrels! Two piccolos! —Two piccolos! Oh what brutes!"

Audiences of the day, accustomed to outbursts of one kind and another at public performances, were indifferent, as a rule, to such trifles and were merely dismayed by the sight of a young man trembling with rage, his fists clenched, his eyes blazing, and his mop of hair waving like a huge umbrella over the beak of a bird of prey. But if a favorite soloist was substituted for, then the entire audience would join the "rebels" in the pit in protest, dashing into the orchestra in pursuit of

Right: *Carl Maria von Weber, 1786–1826*

Below: *Weber conducting Der Freischütz at Covent Garden in London shortly before his death*

the musicians, who ran backstage, and smashing the desks, chairs, and instruments. In the course of such extravagant public demonstrations Hector's pleadings to spare the orchestra's property remained unheeded.

It was during this period, when in his devotion to opera he was feeling both enthusiasm and despair, that Hector heard the first performance of Weber's *Der Freischütz* at the Théâtre de l'Odéon. That the opera was laughed at and even hissed by the audience did not dampen Hector's enthusiasm in the least. Thus far his knowledge of dramatic works had been derived from the classics, and it was surprising even to him that the novelty of Weber's opera, with its nonclassic libretto, could hold such an attraction. Despite the inferior production, he never missed a single performance, until he could almost say that he knew the opera by heart.

The impact on him of *Der Freischütz* led Hector not only to the study of Weber's other works, but to a desire to convey his admiration personally to the composer. But again, he was too shy to write; he knew no one who could have introduced him to Weber, and he missed all three opportunities—at the Opéra, at Lesueur's, and at a music shop—when a "chance" meeting could have come about. A few months later Weber died in London. Berlioz remained his great admirer, and some fifteen years later orchestrated Weber's *Invitation à la valse* and recitatives from *Der Freischütz*, two out of only five compositions which Berlioz ever arranged for orchestra.

Hector must have been inspired by *Der Freischütz*, for in collaboration with his friend Humbert Ferrand, who was to supply him with a libretto, he began an opera, based on a history of the Vehmic Courts in medieval Germany written by François Loeve-Veimars (1801–1854). Hector's opera was to be called *Les Francs-Juges*, but of this second early attempt at an opera only the overture survived, and the best ideas in the score were developed in Berlioz's later works.

Chapter Four

*T*he year 1827 was an ominous one in Hector's life. He was twenty-four and had already experienced his share of disappointments, when he was struck by a passion which he compared to a bolt of lightning. Nobody since his Estelle, whose image was ever present in his subconscious, had disturbed him so emotionally as an English actress he saw as Ophelia in *Hamlet*.

Five years previously, in 1822, an English theater company had been hissed by the Parisians. It was too soon after Waterloo, and in their resentment against the English "invasion" they branded Shakespeare "an aide-de-camp of Wellington." But the wounded national pride had since healed, and Gallic common sense and reasonableness prevailed in lectures and articles by the young French literati, changing public opinion from hostile to appreciative.

It was a *must* for Parisians to attend the series of Shakespearean plays offered by Charles Kemble in September of 1827. And while the audiences were overwhelmed by the performances of the company, Hector was swept off his feet by the leading actress.

Twenty-seven-year-old Harriet Constance Smithson was
born in Ennis, Ireland, on March 18, 1800. She had begun
her stage career at the age of fifteen at the Crow Street
Theatre in Dublin and during the following years appeared
in Ireland, Birmingham, and at the Drury Lane in London.

Although she played for many years in London and in
the English provinces, and even appeared as Desdemona to
Edmund Kean's Othello, Miss Smithson had never been con-
sidered by the English as a first-rate performer. Tall, well-
built, and handsome, she was most noted for her voice, more
distinct than powerful, with a tremulous timbre which gave
especial charm to her expressions of grief and tenderness.

It is not surprising that Hector, the musician, was suscep-
tible to these qualities, especially at a time when his depressed
state of mind made him extremely vulnerable. Miss Smith-
son's Irish accent, which handicapped her success in London,
was unnoticed by the Parisians, and certainly by Hector, who

A Paris boulevard (After a painting by Turner)

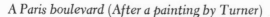

did not know a word of English. His dim understanding of
the spoken words came to him via a rather poor French trans-
lation which, as he discovered later, when he knew some
English, did as little credit to Shakespeare as the English trans-
lations did to Molière and La Fontaine.

Nor was Hector an exception among most of the audience,
who did not realize that Miss Smithson, in her role as Ophelia,
had a sudden lapse of memory in the mad scene. Forgetting
her lines, she walked across the stage as in a trance. She
paused, then began her song without expression. Her veil
fell, she burst into tears, and slowly walked off the stage.
The audience was gripped by a powerful emotion—women
sobbed and men wept or hurriedly left the theater.

But apparently the language barrier was insufficient to
prevent Shakespearean ideas and passions from penetrating
young Hector with such power that the shock from his im-
pressions produced an emotional condition which, as he ob-
served later, only a great sage, learned in the ways of the mind,
could adequately describe. This was a slightly exaggerated
statement, although his behavior following the first perform-
ance was singular indeed.

He became so depressed that he could not work, and kept
wandering about Paris and the neighboring countryside. Some-
times he would fall asleep from sheer exhaustion wherever he
happened to be at the time: one night in a field near Villejuif,
some twenty miles outside Paris, on other nights in the snow
on the banks of the Seine, or on a table in a café on one of
the grand boulevards of Paris, where he would sleep for five
hours while the waiters avoided him for fear that he was dead.

"Inspired," as one might say, by his sufferings, he com-
posed a song based on Thomas Moore's poem from his *Irish
Melodies*: "When he who adores thee . . ." Berlioz was very
fond of this song. Even later in his *Mémoires* he said: "This

is the only occasion on which I have been able to vent any strong feeling in music. And I think that I have rarely reached such a poignant truth of melodic expression, combined with such sinister harmony."

The song in its original version was difficult to sing as well as difficult to accompany. For as long as twenty years afterward Berlioz preferred not to hear it rather than have it badly performed. For a while he contemplated arranging an orchestral accompaniment, but soon gave up the idea. "Works of this nature are not suited for the ear of the concert public," he reflected, "and to expose them to its indifference would be sacrilege." He burned the manuscript.

But Berlioz had an extraordinary capacity for remembering once-conceived melodies, and years later, when he found a suitable translation of Moore's poem, he adapted it to the final version of the song. The *Elégie* was published in 1830 in the collection of his songs called *Irlande*. "If this elegy ever becomes known in England and Germany," Berlioz remarked later, "it may possibly find a few admirers among those who have known grief. But it would remain incomprehensible to most Frenchmen, and be simply insane to an Italian."

Was Berlioz reminiscing about his family's and friends' amusement at his suffering over his Estelle, the young lady with the pink shoes?

After realizing the consequences to his emotional state of the first performance of *Hamlet*, Hector swore to expose himself never again to a similar experience. He could not, however, resist seeing *Romeo and Juliet*, and it merely added fire to his agonized condition. His enthusiasm for Miss Smithson was further stirred by the reviews that he read avidly. To his knowledge no other actress had ever been so acclaimed by the French press.

Hector Berlioz fell desperately in love with Harriet Smithson. Desperately, and hopelessly, for who was he, he kept

Harriet Constance Smithson (Painting by Dubufe)

asking himself, to claim Miss Smithson's attention?—a no-
body, an unknown musician, a student at a conservatory. Per-
haps if he were *somebody*, he thought, if he could show her
that he too was an artist, he would have a better chance.
Guided by this idea, Hector decided to give a concert. This
could not fail, he was convinced, to bring his name to his
heroine's attention, and that would be the first step toward
winning her. He set immediately—and feverishly—to work on
this romantic project, which in addition to the copying of all

the score parts required no small expenditure of energy and diplomacy to obtain an orchestra, soloists, chorus, a conductor, and above all permission to use the concert hall at the Conservatory.

Although Hector must have been well aware of the rather meager number of his compositions, he insisted on having the program of the concert devoted entirely to his works. Since no composer had ever before ventured to do this in Paris, Hector thought that it would definitely make his concert an extraordinary event. And after all, his sole aim was not the money he could earn, but a chance of becoming known—known particularly to Miss Smithson.

The program of the concert on May 28, 1828, included his *Waverley Overture*, a *Mélodie pastorale*, for solo and chorus, taken from *Les Francs-Juges*, the *Resurrexit* from his *Mass*, and the *Francs-Juges* overture. Despite the advance publicity, which through his friends he managed to obtain from the press, the hall was half empty. And what audience there was failed to appreciate his works. But Hector was satisfied. François Joseph Fétis, the eminent critic, whose mere appearance in an audience enhanced any performance, hailed him in his reviews as a genius, thus introducing Hector to his fellow artists and the public in the most flattering terms. "Will the tidings of my success reach Miss Smithson amidst the intoxicating whirl of her own triumphs?" Hector mused. Miss Smithson never even heard of the concert.

Unaware of this, Hector wrote her a letter. He wrote her more than one, but she never replied. Later, when he heard that she was scheduled to appear in two acts of *Romeo and Juliet* at a benefit performance at the Opéra-Comique, he managed (according to his own account) to get one of his works performed on the same program in order to attract Miss Smithson's attention. He came to the rehearsal just as the English actors were finishing, and in time to see *his* Juliet in the arms of another Romeo. Sobbing aloud, he ran out of the theater. "Juliet at last has seen and heard me [he later wrote]. . . . I frightened her, and she has asked the actors who were with her to watch me, *as the look in my eyes warned of nothing good.*"

Miss Smithson, Hector said, never heard his composition at the performance, and in his *Mémoires* he went into a lengthy explanation of why even if she had noticed his piece on the program there would have been slight chance of her paying much attention to it. Even if the composition had been loudly acclaimed she was much too preoccupied with her own performance, and too busy in her dressing room. "And suppose she had heard the composer's name," Hector reflected, "would this have changed her indifference to love?"

It is interesting to note how much Berlioz lived in his imagination, for not a word of this account was true. The composition, which he failed to mention by name, was neither considered for nor given at the performance. Did he see her at a rehearsal, or was that too part of his dream?

The end of his story, however, is more likely to have happened. He had taken lodgings "purely by chance" in a building almost opposite Miss Smithson's apartment. According to Berlioz, the following happened on the day of her departure for Holland:

Hector was depressed and restless and, as he looked out of the window, he caught a glimpse of his "beloved" leaving the house and driving off. "No words can describe what I suffered; even Shakespeare has never painted the horrible gnawing at the heart, the sense of utter desolation and the worthlessness of life, the torturous throbbing of the pulse, and the wild confusion of mind. I stopped composing; my mind became paralyzed as my passion grew I could only suffer."

Thus ends Hector Berlioz's account of the first chapter of his love for Harriet Smithson.

Chapter
Five

*N*ot even a desperate lover can enjoy his suffering forever. But Hector Berlioz was a rare exception. When such a passion suddenly strikes a temperamental being, it is apt to subside just as rapidly, but as in Hector's case the passion was a creation of his fantasy, it remained simmering in his consciousness. Nourished by his imagination the flame was kept alive. Just as his Estelle had been ever present in his mind, so now it was Miss Smithson who came to represent his original Estelle, his *idée fixe*, as he called it.

Fortunately for Hector, he could not devote himself entirely to dreaming about his idol, or about himself as a great composer; he had to face the more prosaic aspects of life and find a way to keep himself alive by means of his chosen profession. As it was, he could talk more about what he intended to do than show what he had done. He was still only a student at the Conservatory. He had developed his own opinions and ideas about music, but he was too anxious to impose them not only on his fellow students but on his professors, who were not always affable about being "given a lesson." Criticism does not always bespeak erudition, and in Hector's case his admonitions were apt to come across as youthful arrogance.

Although his views as regards Weber's compositions and the Beethoven symphonies (recently imported into France) were perfectly sound, it was the way he expressed them that irritated even such well-disposed persons as Lesueur. And by his argumentative insistence on having the last word, he antagonized most of the members of the faculty including Luigi Cherubini, the Conservatory's director, whose influence it was not wise to underestimate. Perhaps without realizing it, Hector was making enemies when what he needed was more friends.

At this time an opportunity to exercise his eloquence in a more realistic, as well as financially profitable, way was offered him by his friend Humbert Ferrand. Ferrand had suggested Hector's writing musical criticisms for the *Revue Européenne*, of which Ferrand was one of the founders.

Hector was reluctant to accept the proposition—his one and only previous attempt at journalism in this field had not proven satisfactory. While, in a controversy that was still raging, the admirers of Rossini were openly criticizing Gluck, Hector's idol, Hector had written to the editor and proprietor of the *Revue Quotidienne*, then a popular periodical, asking him if he would consider publishing his reply to the Rossinists. He promised to "hit fair as well as hard." His offer was accepted, and Hector rubbed his hands in anticipation of the annihilating blows he would deliver to his adversaries. But when he brought his article, the editor shook his head. "It is all true, but you smash everybody's windows; I could not publish such a piece in the *Revue Quotidienne.*"

Eventually Hector learned much about the art of writing and of the etiquette of journalism, and how to restrain the intensity of his musical criticism. It was far more difficult for him to write prose than to compose, but he needed money and he managed to have several articles on Gluck, Spontini, and Beethoven published by the *Revue Européenne* after they had been extensively "doctored" by Ferrand and the editor of the periodical.

While his journalism added a little toward his financial independence, it was not the field of activity for which his father continued his monthly allowance. Hector's one legitimate argument in his dispute with his father was the Prix de Rome, which he counted on winning, and during the following years he repeatedly entered the competition.

But his endeavors to capture the prize during two consecutive years were unsuccessful. Although he certainly knew what kind of composition was expected from a competitor, Hector persisted in interpreting in his own way each subject offered by the jury. One year two jury votes against him reduced his award to a second prize—a laureate crown, a gold medal, and a free pass to all the opera houses—and the following year, in the jury's opinion, he deliberately threw away the first prize he almost won.

It was a foregone conclusion that the winner of the second prize would get the first if he competed again, but Hector's persistence in going his own way merely antagonized the jury, which expected him to learn from his previous experiences. They felt that by composing as he did he was showing the jurors how much he despised them. "You refuse to write like everybody else. Even your rhythms are different. You would invent new modulations, if such a thing were possible," he was told. Hector understood only too well that such admonitions reflected the view, then prevailing in France, that music must be a pleasing art, "not too exciting, not too dreamy, but joyous." This was not Hector's idea of the meaning and purpose of music.

Rather than encourage a young composer with "revolutionary tendencies," the jury refrained from awarding the first

*Hector Berlioz as a
young man*

prize that year, and Hector had to obey his father and return
to La Côte-Saint-André. There, while nursing his disappoint-
ment, he started the *Eight Scenes from Faust,* inspired by his
recent reading of Goethe's work in a French translation. Once
again, his Estelle was revived in his memories, as he passed
the small villa where she used to live, and he composed a
haunting "Gretchen's Song" for the *Faust.* He had the score
published, but despite some flattering remarks by music critics
he recognized many defects in the composition and withdrew
it from circulation. Much later—almost eighteen years later—
he used the best part of the composition for his *The Damna-
tion of Faust,* which became very popular.

At the same time, while at La Côte-Saint-André, Hector
was working on his first symphony. The *Symphonie fantas-
tique* was his first major work, and it has become his most
significant. Hector conceived it as an "episode in an artist's

Ferdinand Hiller

life," and it was indeed considered to be autobiographical. It consisted of five movements: *Reverie, Scenes in the Country, A Ball, March to Execution,* and *Dream of a Witches' Sabbath.* In the largo introduction to the first movement, Hector used the melody which he had composed at the age of twelve after his first meeting with his Estelle; since then this love leitmotiv had reappeared in several of his compositions, and now, as his passion for Miss Smithson was quite well known in Paris, it was attributed to the English actress—his new "Estella montis," Estelle of the mountain, the unattainable.

Berlioz was against printing the programmatic content in the concert programs, for he wished the composition to be accepted as a symphony. To Humbert Ferrand, whose interest and advice he valued, he wrote that he was not in the least guided by a revengeful feeling against Miss Smithson when, in the last movement of the symphony, he wrote a grotesque version of the *idée fixe*, the love leitmotiv. (In this movement the witch is greeted by cries of obscene joy from her fellow demons.) And yet, in the same letter to Ferrand, Hector continued: "She is an ordinary woman, gifted with an instinctive genius for reproducing the wrackings of the human soul without ever having felt them, and incapable of conceiving a mighty and noble sentiment such as that with which I honored her."

Camille Moke

This spiteful statement might have been prompted by Hector's discovery (which he confided to Ferrand) of "frightful truths of which there was no possibility of doubt." Hector had not seen Miss Smithson for a whole year—she was in England. But he had heard some theatrical gossip, utterly unfounded. The fact that Miss Smithson was well guarded by her mother and her hunchback sister from the promiscuities traditionally accorded to the theatrical profession could not assuage Hector's anxiety—for the simple reason that upon his return to Paris, he himself became involved in a love affair whose intricacies could only give proof to his suspicions about feminine fickleness.

It all began when he met and became close friends with Ferdinand Hiller, a nineteen-year-old German pianist and composer, who confided to Hector his love for an eighteen-year-old Parisian, Camille Moke, a talented pianist. The two young men, in addition to music, had much in common. Hiller, like Hector, was "desperately in love," and he told his friend that although at first he had to be content with merely discussing music under the watchful eye of Camille's mother, Camille and he eventually found a way to elude this chaperoning in the distant parts of Paris—a practice which must have supported Hector's lack of faith in Miss Smithson's own guardians of virtue.

The Revolution of 1830 in Paris

Very much impressed by Hector's eloquent descriptions of his feelings toward Miss Smithson, Hiller talked so much about it to Camille that her natural curiosity was aroused. Hiller was too young to realize the challenge he provoked in Camille when he assured her that he, Hiller, would never be jealous of Hector because he knew that Hector would never fall in love with Camille.

At that time, to add to his meager income, Hector was teaching guitar in the girls' school where Camille gave piano lessons. Hector at first paid little attention to the artful looks with which the young lady began her campaign to prove the fallacy of Hiller's statement. But the ardor with which she persisted in her conquest brought the intended result. And as if necessary to remove the last obstacle, to absolve Hector's feelings of loyalty to his young friend, Camille assured him that she was merely fond of Hiller and that their platonic relationship would never lead to anything else.

Blessed by this soothing "go-ahead" sign, Hector gave vent to his passionate nature and for the first time in his life enjoyed an experience which no longer was merely imaginary. The impact of this new experiment was so strong that Hector, overwhelmed, would have asked for Camille's hand then and there had her mother not made it clear that she had planned a far more advantageous future for her daughter than a union with a penniless musician.

But Hector's faith in his fortunes never wavered. Once more, for the fourth and last time—as he swore to himself and his father—he joined the competition for the Prix de Rome. The cantata subject offered to the candidates dealt with the death of Sardanapalus, a king who preferred to destroy himself by fire rather than abdicate. This time Hector's whole future was at stake and he behaved himself. To please the jury he wrote most of the composition in a form expected from a Conservatory pupil. But he reserved all his imagination and skill for an extra final movement, which he planned to add after he had safely won the prize.

Hector had barely finished his composition when on July 29 the Revolution of 1830 broke out in France. Although his sympathies were with the revolutionaries, the three-day-long insurrection was over before Hector could join in it. With a pistol in his pocket, he made his contribution to the cause, relegated to taking part in the crowds of people singing revolutionary songs in the streets—and of all things one of his own songs, *Chant Guerrier*, from his collection *Irlande*. Hector also led the singing of the *Marseillaise*, which he had only recently arranged for a large orchestra and double chorus in a highly dramatized version for "all who have voices, hearts, and blood in their veins!"

With this headline on his manuscript and a dedication to the composer, he ceremoniously dispatched his orchestral version of the *Marseillaise* to Rouget de Lisle, the aging lieutenant of the French Revolution who had written the song some forty years earlier and who now lived in retirement at Choisy-le-Roi.

Five months later Hector heard from Rouget de Lisle, whose *Marseillaise* had meanwhile been adopted as the French national anthem.

"We are strangers, Monsieur Berlioz; shall we become friends?" De Lisle wrote to Hector. "Your head seems to be a volcano in a perpetual state of eruption; there was a straw fire in mine which is burnt out, and has left but a little smouldering smoke. However, the riches from your volcano and the remains of my straw fire combined may yet produce something. So I have two proposals to make to you. But we must see and know each other first. If you care, tell me what day I can see you. . . . I should not have waited this long to make your acquaintance, and to thank you for the honor you have done a certain poor little song in clothing its nudity with your brilliant imagination."

Although Rouget de Lisle did not mention the subject of his second proposal, Hector heard that he wished to show him the manuscript of his opera based on *Othello*. But five months had passed since those turbulent summer days which had ignited Hector's revolutionary enthusiasm, five months during which Hector was so preoccupied with his own life that by the time De Lisle's letter reached him, he apparently was less interested in the old man's proposition. At first he postponed their meeting. And later Rouget de Lisle died before Hector could see him.

Hector's new life began that year (1830) with his winning of the long-coveted Prix de Rome. With it, besides the prestige and the five-year scholarship, he not only made headway in the long-drawn-out argument with his family, but secured independence enough to claim Camille's hand. This decisive step was warranted by Hector's complete faith in the happiness which his marriage to Camille would bring him. His love for her was strong enough to overcome even such trials of his artistic integrity as Camille's criticisms of the slow movements of Beethoven's symphonies and piano sonatas. According to her they were "too slow" and too long. She also irritated him with the "personal pianistic embroideries" with which she freely adorned the pieces she played for him. "All that love offers, all that is most tender and delicate, I have from her," he told Humbert Ferrand. "My enchanting sylph, my Ariel, my life, seems to love me more and more."

But what about Miss Smithson? Camille must have taken good care of this problem. And she did it not by merely teasing him about his one-sided love for the English actress, but by realistically proving to him the difference between imaginary and true love and the advantage of the latter. Still, Hector's happiness did not completely obliterate his passion for Miss Smithson. It only removed him to a distance from which he could more coolly watch her theatrical career being downgraded.

Unrecognized as a first-rate actress in England, Harriet Smithson returned to Paris, where she was reduced to walk-on parts. Hector said that he "pitied her" and was chagrined by the reverses in her career; at other times he spoke of her in harsh terms as "that Smithson wench"—all of which scarcely suggested that Romeo now viewed his Juliet with total indifference.

Since Hector had won the prize, Camille's mother was less of an obstacle to his marriage. Realizing that he would soon be departing for Rome, and that in his absence Camille's love would probably not survive much longer than her previous frequent infatuations, she consented to their engagement. Rings were exchanged, although without the blessing of Hector's parents. They had barely reconciled themselves to the idea of Hector irrevocably becoming a musician and were not

ready to suffer the further blow of Hector's binding his life
to that of an obscure piano teacher, no less the shocking
misalliance with Madame Moke, Camille's mother, who
owned a small lingerie shop in Montmartre in Paris.

But nothing could mar Hector's high spirits. Three con-
secutive events which followed his winning of the Prix de
Rome were of major importance to him: a public performance
of *The Death of Sardanapalus*, the cantata which had won
him the prize, the scheduling of his overture to Shakespeare's
The Tempest for a performance at the Opéra in November,
and the first performance of his *Symphonie fantastique* on De-
cember 5, 1830. The first of these three occasions was to
announce the recognition of Hector Berlioz as a bona fide
composer, the second was to coincide with his betrothal, and
the third would mark a milestone in the beginning of his
musical career. And it mattered little to him later that the
first two were complete failures.

At the rehearsal of the cantata, with the prize in his pocket,
so to speak, Hector produced his extra version of the final
scene—the conflagration in which Sardanapalus, recognizing
his defeat, calls for his prettiest slaves and perishes with them
on the funeral pyre he himself orders built. Hector's realistic
musical description of this scene caused such a sensation at
the rehearsal that at the public performance not a single va-
cant seat could be found in the hall.

"Five hundred thousand curses on musicians who do not
count their bars!" Berlioz cried in his *Mémoires*, as he de-
scribed the unfortunate event. "In my score, the horn gives
the cue to the kettledrums, the kettledrums to the cymbals,
the cymbals to the big drum, and the first sound of the big
drum brings the final explosion. But the damned horn made
no sign, the kettledrums were afraid to enter, and of course
the cymbals and big drum also remained silent; nothing was
heard! nothing!!! And all the time the violins and basses car-

ried on their impotent tremolo, a ridiculous fiasco instead of the climactic end of all things everyone had talked of. No one who has not been through a similar experience can conceive what a fury I was in!"

And indeed, with a cry of horror, Hector flung the score across the middle of the orchestra, knocking down two of the music desks. There was a general uproar in the orchestra and among the scandalized members of the jury, the mystified musicians, and Hector's enraged friends. "This is the most disastrous of all my musical catastrophes," Hector exclaimed.

According to the conditions stipulated by the Prix de Rome,

A contemporary cartoon showing Berlioz conducting his own music

Hector was supposed to leave for Rome, but he delayed his departure for several reasons: he hated to part with Camille so soon after their engagement, he wanted to be present at the performance of his overture to Shakespeare's *The Tempest*, and he was determined to prove the worth of his cantata with a more successful production at the concert in which he was also going to introduce his *Symphonie fantastique*.

On the night of the performance of the overture to *The Tempest*, an unusual storm, a regular "tempest," raged in Paris, preventing most of the audience from reaching the Opéra. It was a great disappointment. Hector fared better with the concert: the cantata, though by no means performed perfectly, as he said, nevertheless created the effect he had been seeking—the conflagration took place and the great crash followed.

And Hector was most pleased with the reception accorded his *Symphonie fantastique*. Spurring controversy, like any new sensation, the work was given both exaggerated praise and unfair and extravagant abuse by the press. Brushing aside the references to his "peculiar" ideas about music in general, Hector paid more attention to the criticisms of some of the defects in the composition. "It took me years," he later said, "to eradicate them from my symphony."

The date of this afternoon concert at the Conservatory happened to coincide with that of a benefit performance for Miss Smithson at the Opéra at seven in the evening. It is doubtful that Hector had planned this. Only those who wished to see a romantic connection between the two events felt gratified as they rushed from the Conservatory to attend the performance at the Opéra. Hector was not among them.

Three weeks later, with a heavy heart, he parted from his fiancée, and, after a brief visit with his family at La Côte-Saint-André, went to Italy.

Chapter
Six

*T*he year and a half—from January 1831 to May 1832— that Hector Berlioz spent in Italy was not, he later claimed, particularly profitable to the further development of his art. It took him some time to acclimatize himself to a new environment and to adjust to life at the French Academy in Rome. The students gave him the customary welcome and Hector was quickly made a part of their extracurricular activities at the Café Corso, a traditional rendezvous for artists from all over the world.

But he was too suddenly torn from Paris, where his emotional and artistic life had only begun to grow roots. Hector was not merely homesick—he was extremely worried because weeks had passed and he still had no word from Camille. Unnerved, he decided to go to Paris to find out what had happened, but he was warned by the director of the Academy that leaving was against the rules of the Prix de Rome and would cause him to forfeit all the privileges due him from the prize. It was a serious threat to everything he had struggled to achieve, as well as to his planned marriage at Easter in

1832. Camille's mother had insisted on this date as a condition of her consent to the engagement.

Hector's anguish over this problem further aggravated his nervous state, provoking another attack of quinsy. But although feverish he managed to work, and had rescored the *Ball Scene* in the *Symphonie fantastique*, and added a coda, when in the middle of April he at last received a letter from Camille's mother. The letter announced Camille's marriage to Camille Pleyel, the wealthy piano manufacturer.

The twenty-nine-year-old Hector instantly made up his mind. He was going to kill all three: the two women and the man who had snatched his bride-to-be. This was his duty, Hector believed. And, as for the disastrous consequences to his own life and career—they mattered little, for he would then commit suicide.

As a first step, he wrote on the score of the *Ball Scene*, the orchestration of which he had not yet completed: "I haven't the time to finish this, but, if the Paris Concert Society should take into its head to perform this work during the *absence* of the composer, I request Habaneck [the conductor] to double the passage for flutes in the bass octave with the clarinets and horns the last time the theme is introduced, and to write the final chords for full orchestra; that will do for the ending."

Having thus written his last testament as far as his art was concerned, Hector carefully thought out and organized in his mind a whole plan of action. He suspected, and with good reason, that his unannounced visit would not be welcome in Camille's home, and he had a seamstress quickly make a chambermaid's dress which would serve him as a disguise.

Then, with two fully loaded double-barreled pistols and two little bottles of laudanum and strychnine in his pockets, he boarded the first mail coach going to France. He stowed away the feminine apparel in one of the side-pockets of the coach.

Jolting along in the seat next to the coachman (who at the

sight of the two pistols refrained from uttering a single word
to his excited passenger), Hector brought into final focus the
dramatic scene toward which his journey was speeding him.

He would go to Camille's home at nine in the evening,
when he knew the family was usually having tea. Dressed as
a chambermaid of the Countess X—he had not yet decided
whose name to use—he would deliver a letter requiring an
immediate reply. Once ushered into the drawing room, he
would wait while Madame Moke opened the letter. Then he
would shoot first her and Monsieur Pleyel; then, after throw-
ing off his disguise, he would seize his beloved by the hair
and, oblivious to her shrieks for mercy, blow out her brains.
Having thus appeased his wounded pride, he would fire the
pistol at his own right temple. Should the pistol misfire, he
would resort to the poison he prudently carried with him.

But on reaching Genoa Hector discovered that his luggage
was minus the most important item of the plot—en route
they had had to change coaches and he forgot to take with
him the chambermaid's dress. Feeling that fate was against
him, Hector tried to drown himself in the sea, only to be
"yanked out like a fish" by a passer-by. The cold bath, how-
ever, did not bring him to his senses, and after equipping him-
self with another chambermaid's dress he proceeded in all
haste to Nice.

Whether it was the harrowing trip along the Corniche
Road (during which each jolt of the coach threatened to
plunge them off a steep precipice into the Mediterranean), or
whether Hector was still tasting the salt water from his recent
attempt at drowning—whatever the cause, his own death, so
essential to his dramatic project, suddenly lost its appeal as
the solution to his problem. In fact Hector felt very sorry for
himself, sorry to "bid farewell to life and art, and to go down
in posterity merely as a fool who could not get along in
the world, and to leave the unfinished symphony and all the

other, greater works, which were seething in [his] brain."

It was fortunate that because of the political situation in France, Hector could not go to Paris except by a roundabout way, that is, via Nice, and that Nice at that time belonged to the Sardinian Kingdom and was Italian territory. Thus Hector in his wild escapade had not actually left Italy, and therefore after writing a *mea culpa* letter to the director of the Academy he was forgiven and allowed to return.

He "convalesced" for three weeks in Nice, a period he later came to consider the happiest days in his life. He sobered up sufficiently to disclose the whole episode to his parents, and he resumed correspondence with his friends in Paris, whom he asked for "musical news." He worked on an overture to Shakespeare's *King Lear*, and also sketched *Lélio*, a mono-drama with words spoken and sung, a work which he called the "Return to a New Life," symbolic of these days when he was on his way back to Rome. His excursion had cost him twelve hundred francs, almost half of his yearly scholarship, but he did not begrudge the high price for his experience—it would have cost far more had he continued his journey.

Upon his return to the Academy no questions were asked and he settled down to a routine life inside and outside of the institute. And as students were free to leave the Academy for travel in Italy, Hector succeeded in seeing as much of the country as he could afford.

One may dislike the Italian way of life, Italian food, climate, or government, theaters, and music, but no man of culture can pass through the cradle of our civilization without being deeply moved and affected by it. And Hector, thanks to his father's tutelage in Latin literature and ancient works of art, fully appreciated the opportunity offered him while in Italy.

He not only enjoyed seeing the great works of art, but could almost feel what inspired them—works of Raphael and Michelangelo, Tasso and Dante. He was thrilled by the sight of Saint Peter's Cathedral, and at the Colosseum he was shaken by thoughts of the tortures of the early Christians. He visited Florence, Milan, Venice, and explored the temples at Pompeii. He never cared for Italian contemporary music or its performance, which he found mediocre—poorly executed by orchestras of too small size. Beethoven and Weber were scarcely known in this country and Mozart's works were never played, though he heard that some people knew something more about the composer than merely that he was a young man of great promise. "The more learned amateurs," Berlioz said, "even knew that he was dead."

No wonder Hector sought no contact with the Italian musicians and was delighted to meet Felix Mendelssohn, who was on his first visit to Italy. Six years younger than Hector, Mendelssohn was at the peak of his career and had already gained a wide European reputation. The two composers had diverse opinions of each other.

Mendelssohn did not take Berlioz seriously as an artist; he thought Hector was "without a spark of talent, looking down from superior heights on Mozart and Haydn and imagining himself to be the creator of a new world while he writes the most horrible things." And Mendelssohn confessed that if

Felix Mendelssohn-Bartholdy,
1809–1847

Hector had not been a Frenchman, with whom life is always agreeable and interesting, he could not have endured his purely external enthusiasm and his vanity. But Mendelssohn's innate good manners did not betray his opinion, and Hector remained his enthusiastic admirer.

In all fairness to Hector, Mendelssohn scarcely knew his work. Hector's co-laureate at the Academy had played on the piano for Mendelssohn some parts of Hector's cantata *Sardanapalus,* and Hector had showed him the first version of the *Symphonie fantastique* and the recently written overture to *King Lear.*

A view of Rome in the nineteenth century

Hector, on the other hand, thought that Mendelssohn was endowed with one of the greatest musical talents of the age and, after Mendelssohn played him Beethoven's sonatas, he became convinced that he was as great a performer as he was a composer.

Unlike Mendelssohn, Hector found no inspiration for his work in Italy. "Music, to the Italians"—and Hector included the Romans, Milanese, Genovese, Florentines, and Neapolitans—"means nothing but an air, a duet, or a trio, well sung. For anything beyond this they feel simply aversion or indifference. Perhaps these antipathies are mainly due to the incompetence of their choruses and orchestras, which effectually prevent their recognizing anything good off the beaten track they have followed so long."

Hector was convinced that to the Italians music was a sensual pleasure and nothing more. "They like music which they can absorb at a first hearing, without reflection or attention," he said, "just like a plate of macaroni."

No wonder that he preferred to roam the countryside, climb mountains, and go hunting—for lack of anything else to do—and to enjoy the company of the simple folk in the villages, for whom he sang and played his guitar, and whose stories took his mind away from the "exile" he was enduring at the Academy.

There was a curious unmusical strain in Hector's character. He liked and sought strenuous physical experiences. He enjoyed hiking through violent storms and climbing dangerous mountain cliffs, as well as listening to the wild escapades with which the "bandits" whom he occasionally met on his excursions regaled him. It was in his extremely passionate nature to like violence, and even the morbid, in everyday life.

Clerical students in front of Rome's Collegio di Propaganda Fide

With his keen observing eye he accumulated a wealth of impressions to nourish his fantasies. He never forgot the wild scenery of the Abruzzi Mountains, "the rugged villagers with their furtive eyes, and their rickety old guns that carry so far and so true," nor the sumptuous monasteries, where pious and kindhearted men welcomed him with their hospitality and surprised him with the charm of their intellectual conversation, nor the Benedictine Abbey of Monte Cassino with its mosaics, wood-carvings, and relics.

But Rome, home of the Church's capital, did not inspire him to a single large religious work all the time he was there. Rome did not make him any more religious than he was before. He became perhaps even more critical of the performed services and was appalled by the abundance of clergy—"Those abbots, monks and priests who are everywhere, right and left, above, below, within and without, with the poor and the rich in church, at dances and cafés, in the theaters, with ladies in cabriolets, on foot with men, in our gardens—everywhere. Where do they all come from?" he gasped.

After a year and a half's absence from Paris, Hector decided to return. His meager accomplishment during his sojourn at the Academy consisted of four compositions. An overture, *Rob Roy*, which he himself considered too long and ineffective, failed a year later in Paris, and Hector destroyed the manuscript. He had rewritten the *Scenes in the Country*, the second movement of his *Symphonie fantastique*. He had completed *Le Chant de Bonheur* for his monodrama *Lélio*, and he had composed *La Captive*, a song inspired by Victor Hugo's *Orientales*.

This song he had composed as if he were indeed a Mozart. While watching a friend of his, an architect, drawing at a table in an inn, Hector had read Hugo's poem. "If I had some music paper, I would write the music to this, for I can *hear* it," he said aloud. The architect obliged by ruling some paper for him, and Hector wrote down an air and sketched the piano accompaniment.

Two weeks later at a musicale given by the director of the Academy, Hector suggested that the man's daughter, who sang, try out his song. He wrote out the piano accompaniment, and the song instantly became popular with the students as well as with the servants of the Academy. Later, realizing its appeal, Hector scored the song for orchestra.

With these compositions Hector seems to have come to the end of his productive capacity in Rome, and he managed to obtain from the director of the Academy permission to leave Italy six months before the end of the required two-year period. To prevent the Paris Academy's knowing what he was doing, he first went to visit his family.

Shortly before he arrived at La Côte-Saint-André he passed Meylan, where had been spent the "happiest hours of my childhood, where I had been thrilled by my first impassioned dreams." He saw in the distance his grandfather's house, and the white villa where Estelle used to spend her summers. Once again his "Estella montis" glimmered against the background of the old rock Saint Eynard.

It was during this visit with his family that Hector's mother played her cruel joke of asking him to deliver a letter to an "old friend" who turned out to be his Estelle. After he recovered from this incident he learned that Estelle had married Casimir Fornier, a Grenoble lawyer and president of the Chamber of Commerce.

Hector spent four months at La Côte-Saint-André, bored with his family, his relatives, and the provincial society. His father tried to persuade him to marry a rich young woman of the neighborhood, but he could not imagine marrying without love. Since the death of his passion for Camille, his heart had remained calm, until he saw Estelle take the letter he brought from his mother.

Part Two

Chapter Seven

*I*n November 1832 Hector arrived in Paris with plans for his future firmly fixed in his mind. Before going to Germany for another year of studies—required by the Prix de Rome scholarship—he wanted to give one or perhaps two concerts in Paris. He intended to return to the apartment on Rue Richelieu where he had lived before going to Italy, but, as the apartment was no longer available, he took one in the house opposite, where Miss Smithson often stayed.

He was told by the porter of the house that only two days before, Miss Smithson had left the very apartment he was taking and had moved to one on the Rue de Rivoli. She was, the porter said, the directress of an English theater which was going to open the following week.

For the past two years Hector had heard nothing about Miss Smithson, who had been in England, Scotland, Holland, and in and out of France. The emotional crisis caused by Camille's sudden desertion had left no place in his heart for a less real Juliet, and now on the day of his return to Paris he was once more reminded of his old passion for the English actress—it could be nothing else but destiny, he concluded.

Hector sensed, however, that if he attended one of her performances, he would fall prey to his feelings and lose the peace of mind he needed to pursue the artistic program he had set for himself. But, he reflected, if after he had successfully completed his concerts he was still drawn to her, he would give up trying to resist temptation and struggle against his fate.

Hector's fortune was otherwise predestined. Two days before his first concert on December 9, 1832, while in the music store of Maurice Schlesinger, his publisher, he noticed an Englishman. After the man had left the shop Schlesinger told Hector that his name was Mr. Schutter and that he was Miss Smithson's close friend. Schlesinger offered, if Hector agreed, to send him tickets to invite Miss Smithson to Hector's concert.

Preoccupied with the rehearsals of his program, Hector was unaware of Miss Smithson's own situation. Contrary to her expectations, the Parisian public was showing practically no enthusiasm for the plays of Shakespeare, which had lost their novelty. Worried over constant financial losses, Miss Smithson could hardly have been expected to be interested in music when Mr. Schutter proposed to take her to the concert, and only after her mother and sister had persuaded her that a little distraction would do her good did she agree to accept the invitation.

She had completely forgotten Hector's name and, naturally, could not ascribe the curious glances and the murmurs from the audience which her appearance in a box right near the orchestra was causing. Nor did the programmatic titles of the *Symphonie fantastique* give her the slightest hint that she was the heroine of "An Episode in an Artist's Life." Not until she saw Hector take his place near the conductor, some ten feet away from her, did Miss Smithson realize this was the man who used to shower her with letters and who she had hoped had forgotten her.

If the passionate music did not convey to her the love messages of her admirer, and if all the clear allusions to the young composer's feelings, whispered to her by Schlesinger, did not convince her of her major role in the composition, the recitative from Hector's *Lélio*, which followed the intermission, certainly left no doubt in her mind that the concert's message was directed at her.

Indeed how could she question it any further when she heard: "Ah, could I but find her, this Juliet, this Ophelia whom my heart is ever seeking! Could I but drink my fill of that mixture of joy and sadness which true love creates, and on an autumn evening, cradled with her by the north wind upon some wild moor, sleep my last sleep in her beloved arms!"

Overwhelmed, Harriet Smithson must have left the hall and gone home in a trance similar to that of some five years before when, as Ophelia, she had forgotten her lines during her first appearance in Paris and had walked off the stage.

Hector reported to his family the "great success" of his concert, the demands for a repeat performance of the *Symphonie fantastique,* and the congratulations from Paganini and Victor Hugo, and he quoted the critics who announced that "this young man will have from now on an audience at his feet." But, well aware of his parents' attitude toward "actresses," he prudently did not mention Miss Smithson's name, thus unfortunately preventing posterity from ever knowing what happened when, on the day after the concert, Hector Berlioz was at long last presented to Harriet Smithson.

It is easy to imagine what followed. "What an improbable romance life is! . . . Yes, I love her, I love her and am loved in return," Hector exclaimed. But the long-coveted love affair did not proceed as smoothly as he had hoped. Hector was determined to marry Miss Smithson and he was impatient over the obstacles which this quick decision created. Both his and Harriet's family were against the match. Hector had to take legal steps to save himself from being disinherited by his father, who gave an emphatic "No" to the matrimonial project. And Harriet's sister argued against Harriet's marrying a young man whose fortunes amounted to two hundred and fifty francs a month from his scholarship, at a time when Harriet herself was fourteen thousand francs in debt.

Hector, however, was far more concerned with Harriet's and his own feelings. The two had successfully overcome the impressions they had had of each other as a result of malicious gossip—Harriet a "frivolous and virtueless actress," and Hector "irresponsible and even epileptic." Hector thought Harriet timid, hesitant, and easily influenced and, although she had accepted his proposal, he was not going to trust his happiness to just an "engagement."

According to the conditions of the Prix de Rome he was expected to go to Germany in January 1833, but Hector had no intention of risking a repetition of what had happened once before when he left behind a fiancée to go abroad. It would be a dangerous gamble with his scholarship, but Hector was willing to face it. He had been asked by the Théâtre Italien to write a comic opera, for which he chose Shakespeare's *Much Ado About Nothing*. And while the actual performance of this work (*Beatrice and Benedict*) had to wait some thirty years, with this project on hand plus several concerts he was in the midst of organizing, Hector felt confident that the Academy would not cancel his Prix de Rome privileges if he delayed going to Germany.

As if to add to their trials, Harriet had an accident. She was

A lithograph portrait of Hector Berlioz

returning from the rehearsal of a benefit performance when, on leaving the carriage at the door of her home, she fell and broke two bones in her leg, just above the instep. It was a calamity. She was ordered to rest in bed to save her from becoming lame and, all the while, the extra expenses from her cure were adding to her debts.

When she refused Hector's immediate assistance of a few hundred francs by threatening never to see him again, he resorted to a more palatable way of helping by turning a performance which she had planned into a concert for her benefit. He managed to secure the participation of Franz Liszt, at that time one of the most popular artists in Paris, and the modest sum from the receipts helped in part to pay some of Harriet's most pressing bills.

Hector had applied to the Ministry of Fine Arts for an advance on his scholarship, but not only was his request refused —he was told to go immediately to Germany. With Harriet still vacillating about taking the final step, the thirty-year-old Berlioz played his last trump card in his game against his reluctant fiancée: he swallowed two tablets of poison in her presence to convince her of the strength of his love. It was more than Harriet could bear. She gave her final consent to marry him. When she then begged for a delay in the ceremony he told her he would leave immediately for Germany and, in fact, applied for a passport.

They were married at the British Embassy in Paris on October 13, 1833. "Harriet's fortune consisted of fifteen thousand francs of debts; my property—of three hundred borrowed francs and a fresh quarrel with my parents. . . . But she is mine, and I defy the world," said the happy bridegroom.

Chapter Eight

*D*uring the following four years Berlioz was harassed by what seemed to be a hopeless financial situation. He did succeed in getting the Ministry of Fine Arts to exempt him temporarily from going to Germany—his recent success enabled him to claim that his presence in Paris was imperative to his career as a composer. And as soon as Harriet had partly recovered, he organized another benefit performance at the Théâtre Italien.

The evening's program was divided into two parts, dramatic and musical. In the first, Madame Marie Derval scored such a success in Alexander Dumas' *Antony* that Harriet's performance of Ophelia's scene in the fourth act of *Hamlet* was barely applauded. But the worst happened during the second part of the program. To spare the expense of hiring the orchestra from the Opéra, Berlioz had made an arrangement with the director of the theater to use the theater's musicians, merely supplementing them with a few from the Opéra orchestra. As the theater musicians were not paid for extra performances, they showed no particular interest in playing, and certainly not in an alliance with members of the Opéra orchestra who *were* paid. Nevertheless, under Berlioz's own conducting the *Francs-Juges* overture was applauded, and Liszt's brilliant performance of Weber's *Concertstück* was given an ovation.

But this was only the beginning of the concert. Next on the program was the *Sardanapalus* cantata. Berlioz, at best still a far from experienced conductor, and unnerved now by every-thing that had already happened, missed giving a cue to the second violins in the orchestral introduction, thus so upsetting the whole performance that he had to skip the rest of the composition and call for the final chord.

It was getting late—the concert half of the program had not gotten under way until after eleven o'clock—and since the theater's musicians were not obliged to play after midnight, one by one they left their desks while Berlioz was conducting one of Weber's choruses. And so, when he came on stage again to conduct the final number, the *Symphonie fantas-tique*, Berlioz found himself left with five violins, two violas, four basses, and one trombone, an ensemble hardly sufficient for a performance of the symphony. The audience, however, had no intention of leaving and called for the *March to Execution*. Pointing to the remnants of the orchestra, Berlioz had to close the performance with apologies to the house.

The lack of funds which had forced Berlioz to perform under such makeshift conditions had led to an unprece-dentedly disgraceful occasion, which his gloating enemies hastened to ascribe to "Berlioz's music that drove musicians off the stage."

Harriet was no less distressed than he. Her Ophelia act not only failed to create the impression she had hoped for, but convinced her that her lameness was marring the certainty and freedom of her movements on stage. As much as Berlioz would have liked to arrange another comeback for Harriet, he

was afraid of a repetition of the same, and instead, after pay-
ing some debts from the two thousand francs the unfortunate
performance had brought him, he organized a concert of his
own works.

This time disregarding the expense, he amassed for his or-
chestra the "very elite of Paris musicians." It proved to have
been worth it, not only because the *Symphonie fantastique*
was given an ovation, but because of the enthusiasm of one
of the listeners who came to see Berlioz a few weeks later.

Berlioz had never before met Niccolò Paganini. Several
years back, while he was "returning to a new life," after the
abortive escapade that had taken him from Rome as far as
Nice, Berlioz had passed through Genoa and there had tried
to get information about the virtuoso who was causing such
a stir in Paris, Germany, and England. But the commercially
minded Genovese spoke indifferently about their distinguished
townsman and could not even show Berlioz Paganini's home.

"I have a wonderful viola," Paganini now told Berlioz, "an
admirable Stradivarius, and I would like to play it in public.
But I have no music for it. Would you write me a solo?"

Berlioz was very flattered, and he immediately began a
composition in which the viola had an important role while
nevertheless remaining a part of the orchestral composition.
When Paganini saw the first movement he was disappointed.
"That is not at all what I want," he said. "I am silent a great
deal too long. I must be playing the entire time."

"What you really want is a concerto for viola," Berlioz said,
"and you are the only man who can write it."

But Paganini said that he was too ill to compose. In fact
suffering from a tuberculosis of the throat which was to ulti-
mately prove fatal, he went to Nice and did not return to
Paris until three years later.

Berlioz, however, once he had started a composition, was
not going to throw it into a wastebasket. Now for the first

time his impressions from his long wanderings in the Abruzzi Mountains bore their fruit. He composed a series of scenes for orchestra in which the viola was to represent an observer, a sort of dreamer in the style of Byron's *Childe Harold*. The composition, to which he gave the title of *Harold in Italy*, was completed with remarkable speed, and its first performance was arranged for November 23, 1834.

Having so recently spoiled the performance of *Sardanapalus* through his own inexperience in conducting, Berlioz this time entrusted Monsieur Girard, the conductor at the Théâtre Italien, with leading the orchestra. But Girard gave a far from satisfactory performance. He became confused by the changes in tempo, and when the audience called for the *Pilgrims' March* (one of the scenes) to be repeated, he failed to help the harpist, who had lost his place, and ended up having to quickly guide the orchestra to the end of the piece, omitting some fifty bars.

The Paris press ridiculed the composition: "Ha, ha, ha! Haro! Haro!—Harold!" And an anonymous letter full of vin-

"Childe Harold's Pilgrimage" (*Painting by Turner*)

dictive and coarse insults reproached Berlioz for lacking the courage to blow out his brains.

Meanwhile his financial situation was not improving. Harriet's debts were still far from being paid, and the family expenses, which already included support of Berlioz's mother-in-law, had been further increased by the birth of a son on August 14, 1834. "He is not named Hercules, John-Baptist, Caesar, or Alexander [the Great], but quite simply—Louis," the happy father wrote to his sister Nanci.

The Berlioz family, alienated by his marriage to Harriet, sent congratulations and a few presents, but gave no sign of financial assistance. Berlioz had already obtained from the Ministry of Fine Arts the scholarship allowance due him for the year 1834: the first half—fifteen hundred francs—in the middle of January, when he declared that he was on the point of going to Germany, and the remaining half in June, granted him because the authorities took into consideration that Harriet was expecting a child. But this money had all been spent, along with the small sums he received for his occasional articles for periodicals. His only chance of substantially improving the situation was to gain a firm foothold at the Opéra; success there would both spread his fame as a composer and remunerate him well.

It was a goal well worth considering, and Hector managed diplomatically to gain the good graces of François Bertin, the director of the Opéra, by helping his daughter with her composing of an opera, *La Esméralda*. It is unimportant how much Berlioz "helped" the young lady with the technical problems of composition, how much he actually wrote himself, or of how much value was his supervision of the rehearsals. He swore that he was merely Mademoiselle Louise Bertin's "musical secretary," that he considered her one of the ablest women of the time, and that her score, while occasionally showing her lack of professional training, had nevertheless many very fine qualities. Mademoiselle Bertin's opera was not a success, but Berlioz had achieved what every composer in France strove for—a commission for an opera. He chose Benvenuto Cellini, the Renaissance artist, as his subject, and he asked Auguste Barbier, a French poet, to write the libretto. For three months in the summer of 1836 he worked incessantly on the opera, but its first performance in 1838 brought another disappointment. It failed and after three more performances was taken off the billboards.

Meanwhile Berlioz received another commission from the Ministry of Fine Arts. He was asked to write a requiem to be performed at the annual commemoration for the victims of the Revolution of 1830. A requiem was one of the subjects close to Berlioz's heart and he set to work composing at such speed that he had to invent a type of shorthand to avoid forgetting the ideas which assailed him.

His score was completed, the parts were copied, and Berlioz had begun the rehearsals when suddenly he was informed that the planned ceremony was to be performed without music. Fortunately for his requiem, however, a general had just been killed at the siege of Constantine in Algeria, and the War Department decided it would use the work at a service for the fallen general and his men.

The service took place on December 5, 1837, in the Church of the Invalides. The solemnity and the drama of the setting were perfectly suited to the composition. Hundreds of people crowded into the Chapel of Saint Louis, whose walls and windows were draped in black. Six hundred candles around the coffin and four thousand other dim lights contributed to the gloomy atmosphere of the domed edifice. A cortege with twenty-four muffled drums representing twelve Paris legions opened the ceremony.

As applause or other loud expression of audience reaction is not permitted in a church, it was impossible to judge

Lithograph by Fantin-Latour honoring Berlioz's Requiem

whether the spectators were overwhelmed, or bored, by Berlioz's *Requiem,* but with the press the composition definitely scored a tremendous success. Thus, at last, Berlioz was recompensed for his years of labor. Not financially, however.

According to the original agreement the government was to allow fourteen thousand francs for the project, plus expenses for the copying of the score parts, and in addition a fifteen-hundred-franc bonus for the composer. But then the sum dwindled to ten thousand francs, and while the chorus, soloists, and copyist were waiting for months to be paid, Berlioz ran from one government department to another only to be told that the assigned sum had been spent on something else. Eventually he succeeded in having everybody paid but himself, and when he asked for three thousand francs for his fee, he was offered instead a Cross of the Legion of Honor. This he refused, and insisting that the three thousand francs be paid immediately, he threatened to publish a full account of the treatment he had received. The sum was paid him, and three months later he was awarded the Cross of the Legion of Honor.

Neither the Cross of the Legion of Honor (which, as he said to the Minister of Fine Arts, was worth two cents to him) nor the three thousand francs, which had all been spent in advance, brought any change in Berlioz's financial situation. In order to complete the score of *Benvenuto Cellini*, he had borrowed two thousand francs, and the disastrous first performance had dashed his belief that he was already firmly established at the Opéra.

However, Berlioz did hear that Paganini, who had returned to Paris, had attended the performance and afterward had said: "If I were manager of the Opéra, I would at once commission that young man to write me three such operas. I would pay him in advance and would make a capital bargain by it."

As Berlioz had no intention of fulfilling the Prix de Rome requirement by going to Germany for further studies, his scholarship was terminated. His only assured income now came from the salary he received as music critic for the *Journal des Débats*, thanks again to the good offices of Monsieur Bertin. In addition to this he received one hundred francs per article from various periodicals—all of which, put together, was not enough to support him and his family, and certainly was not sufficient for his always costly concert projects.

Nevertheless Berlioz gave two concerts that season at the Conservatory Hall. An attack of bronchitis prevented him from conducting the first one on November 25, 1838; the proceeds barely covered the expenses. But despite his illness he insisted on conducting the second performance on December 16, when to attract the public's interest he put the *Symphonie fantastique* and *Harold in Italy* on the same program.

Again Paganini was present. And after hearing for the first time *Harold in Italy*, which was indeed the offspring of his suggestion to Berlioz to write him a piece for viola, Paganini was so impressed that he got down on his knees before Hector while congratulating him backstage.

It was a dramatic gesture, one worthy of Paganini's reputation. The tall slender figure with the prominent aquiline nose, sharp dark brown eyes, and large high forehead framed by locks of raven-black hair was usually seen on stage (otherwise Paganini seldom appeared in public) dressed in a wrinkled frock coat and trousers, and with what was visible of his short collar and tie looking as if he had slept in them. His appearance was more frightening than pleasing but it perfectly befitted the "Paganini legend," which was based on scant knowledge of his mysterious life.

Niccolò Paganini paying tribute to Berlioz at the Paris Conservatory (After a sketch in oils by Yvon)

Niccolò Paganini,
1782–1840

According to some rumors, as a young man Paganini was sent to prison for twenty years for killing his mistress, and there learned to play on one string—a stunt with which he later dumbfounded his audiences. His incredible virtuosity, it was whispered, could only have been acquired from the devil.

During the early years of the century he was famous in Italy and at one time was court musician at Lucca to Elisa Bacciochi, Napoleon's sister. From time to time, however, he would suddenly resign his post and retire from public life to devote himself to the further perfection of his art. Now nearing fifty, he undertook long concert tours through Germany, England, and France, but as he no longer felt the necessity for practicing his violin before concerts, he would remain lying on a sofa for hours, sometimes strumming a mandolin.

He seldom attended musical performances, and his presence at Berlioz's concert was an event in itself. Honored by his tribute, in fact overwhelmed and weakened by emotion, on his way home Berlioz caught a cold which, added to his bronchitis, further aggravated the state of his health.

Two days later Paganini's son brought Berlioz a letter from his father.

"My dear friend," Paganini wrote in Italian, "Beethoven is dead, and Berlioz alone can revive him. I have heard your divine composition [*Harold*], so worthy of your genius, and I beg you to accept, in token of my homage, twenty thousand francs, which will be remitted to you by the Baron de Rothschild on presentation of the enclosed."

The "enclosed" was a two-sentence note in French:

"Sir,

"Be so kind as to remit to Monsieur Berlioz the sum of twenty thousand francs, which I left with you yesterday.
                              "Yours [etc.], Paganini."

Had Berlioz not been confined to bed by his illness, he would have run to thank Paganini for his noble gesture. Instead, all he could do was send a written reply, which Berlioz considered such an inadequate expression of his feelings that he felt ashamed to quote it in his *Mémoires*.

"Great and worthy artist," Berlioz wrote to Paganini, as soon as he finished reading his letter, "how can I express my gratitude! I am not rich; but believe me, the approval of a man of such genius as yours touches me a thousand times more deeply than the royal generosity of your gift.

"Words fail me; I will hasten to embrace you as soon as I can leave my bed to which I am still confined today."

The news of Berlioz's fortunes spread quickly in Paris, and malicious gossip followed. Berlioz's enemies attributed Paganini's gesture to an investment in personal publicity, as

Paganini was assumed to be a miser who would not be so reckless unless he foresaw reaping considerable profit from his assistance to an illustrious musician. There were some who were inclined to believe that the gift came originally from François Bertin, who was by then well known for his patronage of Berlioz, and who might have preferred to remain incognito this time.

This ungallant attitude toward gallant behavior would have marred Berlioz's happiness had Paganini himself not assuaged his annoyance when six days later Hector called on him at his apartment. He found Paganini bending over a billiard table practicing shots. "Don't speak of it. No, not another word," Paganini said to Hector. "It is the greatest pleasure I have ever felt in my life. You will never know how your music affected me. And now, none of the people who intrigue against you will dare say another word, for they know that I am a good judge, and that I am not easy." Paganini spoke French, and Berlioz did not know what he actually meant by his last phrase: *"Je ne suis pas aisé"* could have meant "I am not easily moved by music," or "I don't give my money easily," or "I am not in easy circumstances." (Many years later—in 1854 and 1856—long after his father's death, Paganini's son put an end to the speculation over the identity of Berlioz's benefactor by emphatically stating that the gift was his father's token of admiration for Berlioz.)

Now, at last, Berlioz was free to devote himself to composing. He thought of writing a symphony with chorus and vocal soloists based on Shakespeare's *Romeo and Juliet*. He spoke about it to Paganini, and even wrote him several times at Nice, where Paganini had gone because of his declining health. But Paganini replied that he was too ill to advise him, and he was not destined to hear the work, for a year later he died, on May 27, 1840.

Chapter Nine

*I*t took almost eight months of working day and night for Berlioz to complete his new symphony. Conducted by him, it was performed with great success three times: on November 24, December 1, and December 15, 1839—unprecedented proof of the symphony's popular appeal. With the *Romeo and Juliet Symphony*, Hector Berlioz, as predicted by Paganini, at last firmly established his reputation as a great composer. Berlioz would have had every reason to rejoice, if his personal life had brought him as much happiness.

He had believed that with his success his family would applaud his faith in his chosen vocation, sympathize with the long years of struggle, and be gratified and proud of his achievements. But such was not the case. Their attitude toward him had changed somewhat, but not perceptibly. Except for his younger sister Adèle, they barely corresponded with him.

They had shown some acceptance of Harriet as their daughter-in-law with the small presents they had sent on the birth of her son, but they had offered no financial assistance when

Nanci Berlioz

Hector was in desperate need of it. Hector had to keep from Harriet the letter in which Adèle expressed her hope that time would efface the provincial prejudices against his marriage.

Nanci adhered to her parents' attitude. Hector knew nothing of Nanci's husband, Camille Pal, a Grenoble judge, except that he also had joined in his wife's snobbish conduct toward Harriet. Accepting it good-humoredly Hector referred to the couple as "Their Royal Highnesses."

When in January of 1838 Hector heard of his mother's ill health, his natural impulse was to hasten to her bedside. "I long for you tenderly," he wrote her. But Maria Berlioz

Adèle Berlioz

died the following month, at the age of fifty-three, without his having seen her again.

His father's health now worried him too, and Hector himself was far from being well. The many years of frustration in seeking acceptance for his work, the strain of rehearsals and performances, and the financial problems that gave him frequent insomnia—all had taken a considerable toll on his nervous system. He badly needed rest and comfort, but where was he to find it?

It was hard for Harriet to accept the inevitable—her theatrical career was finished. Hector tried over and over again to find her an opportunity for a new stage appearance, but playing with the amateur English actors would not have constituted the "comeback" she desired, and her foreign accent stood in the way of her acting in French plays. Her failure was not only a blow to her self-esteem, but marked her incompetence in sharing Hector's struggles to subsist. She, who since her adolescence was used to supporting her mother and sister, now felt that she was an extra burden to her husband.

Harriet was not a musician, not even an amateur of music, and she lacked sufficient understanding of her husband's work. This, plus her inadequate knowledge of the French language, made it difficult for her to take part in the musical discussions Berlioz held with the friends who occasionally gathered at their home. It was also hard for her to get used to her new role of housewife and mother.

The years were passing, and Harriet was growing older. She was nearing forty. Only three years her husband's senior, she seemed much older than he. She was losing her looks, getting stout, and becoming careless of her appearance; and, embittered by her failure, she drank more than was good for her.

In the beginning, their romance was nourished by Hector's overpowering passion. Now, five years later, it was Harriet's passionate love, with its possessiveness, that tormented her husband, for Hector's love for her was cooling off. Some peculiarities in Harriet's character that had before either escaped Hector's notice, or were overlooked by him, now became sources of irritation far out of proportion to their importance.

Berlioz, like his father, was a freethinker. He abhorred particularly the routines and rituals associated with religious fervor, and he was seriously disturbed when Harriet, on learning of Paganini's gift, called in their five-year-old boy to join her in prayer. "Come here! Come with your mother," she cried. "Come and thank God for what He has done for your father." They knelt in prayer, the boy obviously ignorant of what it was all about, joining his little hands beside her. "O Paganini! What a sight. . . . What would you say if you saw it?" Berlioz shook his head in bewilderment.

He sympathized with his wife's artistic plight; he was as much devoted to her as before—but that was not what Harriet desired and apparently expected. Her imperative wooing merely embarrassed her husband.

Berlioz too yearned for love, but no longer for Harriet's. It was his need to be always "in love with somebody." He had often told Harriet about his Estelle. She did not take his "childish infatuation" seriously—it merely amused her. But Berlioz often dreamed of Estelle, and one of his dreams, which repeated itself twice, left him disturbed. He dreamed that he was in Meylan. He was alone, sitting under a weeping acacia in the garden of the white villa that he remembered so well. But Estelle was not there and he kept asking himself, "Where is she—where is she?"

In those days, long before Sigmund Freud and Carl Jung, people troubled by their dreams did not seek psychoanalytic aid for their interpretation. Berlioz had to be content with his own reasoning. "Who can explain it?" he said. "Perhaps a sailor could, or the learned men who have studied the movements of the magnetic needle [compass] and know that those of the human heart are much the same."

Harriet had not been jealous of this imaginary love of Hector's, but she became fiercely so when she grew suspicious of Hector's awakened feelings for other women. And in trying to discover the identity of the one who she imagined stood in the way of Hector's passion for her, she made the mistakes usually made by all women in these situations, which only further alienated him. There is no doubt that at the Opéra,

among the singers and members of the ballet, and among the
actresses at the Théâtre Italien, Berlioz had before him an
ample selection of feminine charms. And Harriet, searching
for evidence, not only went through his closets to examine his
suit and coat pockets, but tried to conjecture, from fragments
of letters she intercepted or found in the drawers of his desk,
the object of his affections. She even carefully scrutinized the
articles he wrote for periodicals, hoping to find in them some
clue.

But this rather sorry practice only further beclouded her
mind, for no sooner did she feel that she had obtained suffi-
cient proof of his infidelity than Hector managed to outdis-
tance her discovery by an affair with his next paramour, and
so could protest his innocence.

Harriet felt wretched, and in her jealousy created violent
scenes which spelled the beginning of the end of Hector's
matrimonial happiness. For a long time, to avoid provoking
her outbursts, he had been refusing every occasion for leaving
Paris, even though his short absences from home would have
been in the interest of his musical activities. By 1840, however,
the strained relationship with his wife reached the point where
Hector no longer paid any attention to her tantrums. But he
further complicated the situation by going abroad "not alone,"
as he said, and involving himself in a love affair which, as it
was not in his nature to take an affair as a passing fancy,
finally broke his bondage to Harriet.

Berlioz was convinced that he could help insure permanent
recognition in Paris as a great composer by his success abroad,
and he accepted an engagement for two concerts in Brussels.
He was referring to this journey to Belgium when he said
that he was traveling "not alone." His companion was Marie
Geneviève Martin, the daughter of a French father and a
Spanish mother.

Berlioz had met her in 1841. The twenty-seven-year-old

Harriet Smithson Berlioz

Marie had the fortune to be endowed with a shapely, graceful figure which contrasted poignantly with Harriet's. That was enough to stir Berlioz's passion. It was unfortunate, however, that the young woman was also endowed with a voice and with a great ambition to become an opera star under the stage name of Marie Recio.

While Berlioz was absorbed in her physical charms, Marie's mother encouraged her daughter's liaison with the man who was a much-talked-about composer and music critic and who seemed to have connections at the Opéra—attributes not to be overlooked in the promotion of her daughter's career. And indeed, as a fair price for his courtship, Berlioz succeeded in getting Marie a debut at the Opéra on November 5, 1841, as Ines in Donizetti's *La Favorita*.

As a singer she was a dismal failure but thanks to Berlioz's friendship with some critics her pleasing appearance, rather than her performance, was given the most attention by the press. Berlioz himself, reviewing her second and last appearance in Rossini's *Le Comte Ory*, made the fatal mistake of contrasting her graceful figure with the rather large proportions of Madame Stoltz. Madame Stoltz was the favorite of the new director of the Opéra, and she used her influence to revenge herself against Hector.

Berlioz's reputation as an artist suffered a little as a result, and was done further injury by Marie's insistence on her "cooperation" in his musical projects. Berlioz was neither blind nor deaf in his love. He could hear better than anybody else the inadequacy of Marie's voice and musicianship for the career she aspired to, but he could not resist her physical charms, and he took her with him to Brussels.

Carrying out his scheme to have his success abroad well publicized in the Paris press, he supplied his friends, the critics, with detailed reports of his concerts. It was a simple matter for Harriet, who read about Marie's participation in Hector's programs, to put two and two together so that upon his return home, Hector could no longer escape her well-founded recriminations.

But this time, to her understandable chagrin, she learned that it was not Marie who had intruded into her happiness, but rather that it was she herself who was in Hector's way. It is a matter of conjecture about how amicably Hector and Harriet resolved their problem, but from then on they separated, leaving Berlioz with the burden of keeping up two homes.

Chapter Ten

*B*erlioz felt that he should continue his road to fame by going to Germany, where he had some friends who, he thought, could be helpful to him. Ferdinand Hiller, whose fiancée, Camille, Berlioz had abducted, was living in Frankfort, one of the cities on Berlioz's itinerary. The Camille affair had not disturbed Hiller's friendship with Berlioz. He was well revenged by Camille's desertion of Hector and her marriage to Pleyel. And since then the two friends were merely amused when they read in the Paris papers that Pleyel was suing his wife for divorce because of her too frequent infidelity.

Felix Mendelssohn was in Leipzig as the head of the famous Gewandhaus Orchestra, and Berlioz was sure that Mendelssohn would remember him from the days they had spent together in Rome. But before going to Leipzig he hoped to see Franz Liszt in Weimar.

Berlioz's friendship with Liszt was, on an artistic basis, more intimate than with the other two musicians. Liszt was among the few who were enthusiastic about the first public

*Marie
Geneviève
Martin (Recio)*

performance of his Prix de Rome cantata *Sardanapalus* (following the disastrous rehearsal at which everything had gone wrong and Berlioz had knocked down two musicians' desks by throwing his score on the stage). To express his admiration for the composition Liszt had called on Berlioz the following day, and their first meeting led to a friendship which had grown, as Berlioz said, in warmth and depth ever since.

As a concert pianist Liszt was influenced by Paganini and Chopin, but as a composer he was even more influenced by Berlioz. But since the mid-1830's Liszt had been concertizing constantly throughout Europe—it was his so-called *Glanz-Periode* (period of splendor)—and, as Liszt seldom visited Paris, the two musicians kept in touch by frequent correspondence.

Accompanied by Marie, Berlioz left Paris in the early part

of December, 1842. On their way to Germany they revisited Brussels, where the first concert of the long tour had already been announced by the Society of the Grande Harmonie for December 10. It was postponed for the seventeenth and finally canceled because of the illness of the prima donna who was to take part in it and who was a favorite with the public of Brussels. It was not a successful beginning to Berlioz's tour, and he fared no better in Frankfort.

In the presence of the concert manager, who had engaged Berlioz for two performances, the director of the orchestra told Hector that he had written him not to come. There were two girl violinists who were drawing large crowds in Frankfort, and they had priority on the dates reserved for Hector's concerts. Why did Monsieur Berlioz not remain another day in town, the two men suggested, naïvely trying to comfort him, and see their production of Beethoven's *Fidelio*—he would certainly enjoy it.

At last, in Stuttgart, Berlioz managed to give a concert— with an orchestra much too small for the *Symphonie fantastique* and *Harold in Italy*, and for an audience much too small to cover expenses. He also gave two more concerts, one in Mannheim and the other in Hechingen, but while in his report to his Paris friends he exaggerated his success, Berlioz had already had enough of Marie's participation in his programs.

"She sings like a cat," he wrote Hiller. "That in itself would not matter; the trouble is that she wants to appear in all my concerts." Thus Hector resorted to a ruse. He was going to Weimar, where he could not present Marie, his mistress, to the French ambassador stationed there. He smuggled his luggage out of the hotel to the stagecoach station. Then he told Marie that he was going to spend the evening with Baron de Rothschild, the banker, and he left a letter containing enough money for her fare back to Paris, which the hotel clerk was to deliver to Marie several hours after the departure of the stagecoach.

Berlioz, however, underestimated Marie's resourcefulness. It was a simple matter for her to obtain his destination from the stagecoach station, and instead of buying a ticket for Paris she followed him to Weimar. There she arrived in time to intercept Hiller's letter congratulating Berlioz on his escape from his captivity by Marie. "In lofty tones," Marie herself answered the letter, but poor Berlioz had to add a few humble words, saying that he was neither "captured" nor "recaptured" but happily reunited with Marie.

"Condole with me," he wrote to a friend in Paris. "Marie insisted on singing at Mannheim, Stuttgart, and Hechingen. The first two times it was tolerable, but the last. . . . And at the mere thought of my having another singer she is up in arms." Berlioz had to resign himself to the inevitable—Marie was to sing at his concerts as often as she chose.

Liszt was not in Weimar—he was on his concert tour. And besides, there was no use in complaining about his mistress to Liszt, who was sensible enough to keep his amours off the concert stage. Instead, Berlioz reported to him on the more

Franz Liszt performing in concert

professional difficulties that had made his tour a dismal failure.

"You, my dear Liszt," he wrote him, "know nothing of such uncertainties; it matters little to you whether the town has a good orchestra, whether the theater is available, etc. You can say with complete confidence: 'I myself am orchestra, chorus, and conductor. I can make my piano dream or sing at will, echo with exalting harmonies, and perform with a swiftness to rival the most skillful bow. Like an orchestra it can throw on the evening breeze a cloud of fairy-like chords and vague melodies. Give me a large room and a grand piano, and I am at once master of a great audience; I have but to appear before it to be overwhelmed with applause. My memory awakens; from my fingers flow dazzling fantasias evoking enthusiastic acclamations. I have but to play Schubert's *Ave Maria* or Beethoven's *Adelaide* to draw every heart to myself, and make each one hold his breath.'

"The silence speaks; the admiration is intense and profound . . . ," Berlioz continued his letter. "Then come the fiery shells, a veritable bouquet of fireworks—the acclamations of the public; flowers and wreaths showered upon the priest of harmony as he sits quivering in his chair, beautiful young women kissing the hem of his garment with tears of sacred frenzy; the sincere homage of the serious, the feverish applause wrung from the envious, the intent faces, the narrow hearts amazed at their own expansiveness.

"And the next day the inspired young genius departs, leaving behind him a twilight of dazzling glory and enthusiasm," Berlioz concluded as if he were reviewing to Liszt one of the virtuoso's own performances. "It is a dream; it is one of those golden dreams that come to one whose name is Liszt or Paganini. But the composer who, like myself, must travel to make his works known, has on the contrary to steel himself to a task which is never ending, always beginning, and always unpleasant."

And Berlioz described to his friend the tortures of the re-
hearsals, the cold glances of the musicians which seemed to
say, "What does this Frenchman want? Why doesn't he stay
at home?" and always the lack of proper instruments needed
for performing his compositions.

He did confess, however, the satisfaction he derived from
conducting after all the preliminary work was done—prelimi-
nary work involving his marking the music sheets with the
German notations instead of the French, his often transposing
an English horn solo to the oboe range because the former
instrument was unavailable, and endless rehearsals with chorus
and soloists separately as well as with individual sections of
the orchestra.

"Ah but," Berlioz wrote disclosing his own feelings, "when
the hall fills, the clock strikes, then the composer appears at
his desk, pale and exhausted, scarcely able to stand, uncertain,
faint, and discouraged, until the applause of the audience, the
spirit of the performers, and his own love for his work trans-
forms him into an electric machine, giving forth marvelous
radiations, invisible to be sure, but none the less real. And
then his compensation begins. Ah then, I grant you, the com-
poser-conductor has a life unknown to the virtuoso! With
frantic delight he abandons himself to the pleasure of *playing
on the orchestra!*

"With what magical influence does he sway that magnifi-
cent instrument! Once more his attention embraces every-
thing; his eye is everywhere; with a glance he signals voice and
instrument their entries; with his right arm he flings forth
terrible chords that burst in the distance like harmonious
projectiles; then on a *fermata* he arrests all this movement,
rivets the attention of all, suspends every arm, every breath,
listens for a moment of silence . . . and then gives freer scope
than ever to the whirlwind he has subdued.

"And in grand adagios," Berlioz went on, "how happy he

is, rocked gently on his lovely lake of harmony, listening to the multitude of blended voices singing his love songs or confiding to the solitude of the night his laments for the present and his regret for the past. Then often, but then only, does the composer-conductor forget the public altogether; listening to himself, judging himself, and touched by the emotion which is shared by the artists around him, he takes no further heed of the impressions produced upon the audience far away behind him. If his heart has been thrilled by contact with poetic melody, if he has felt that secret fervor, the herald of the soul's incandescence, his object is attained, the heaven of art is opened to him . . . and what matters earth?

Franz Liszt,
1811–1886

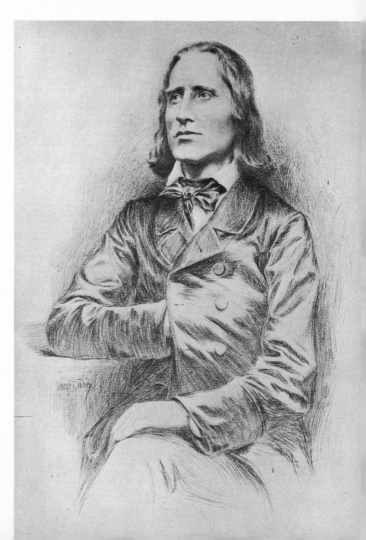

"Then, when all is over, and success assured, his delight is intensified a hundredfold, since it is shared by all his men in their gratification and self-esteem. You, you great virtuosi, are king and princes by the grace of God; you are born on the steps of the throne, while composers have to fight, to overcome and conquer in order that they may reign. But the very labors and dangers of the struggle only enhance the splendor and intoxication of their victory, and they might, perhaps, be even happier than you, had they always soldiers at their command."

Thus ended Hector Berlioz's letter from Weimar to Franz Liszt.

A hundred and twenty-five years ago Germany had no railway system such as we know today, and during his travels across the country, from one large city to another, and with many side trips to smaller towns, Berlioz not only suffered physically from the discomforts of journeying by stagecoach, but also financially because of the expense of the close to five hundred pounds of excess luggage in which was contained his scores and orchestral parts. Nevertheless, though his one year of touring Germany did not bring him a fortune, he was able at times to send an extra two or three hundred francs to Harriet.

If his artistic success was not always as great as he claimed in his reports to Paris, he had definitely reaped many advantages from his journey. He had gained an intimate knowledge of the musical life in Germany—not only the level of the public's interest in and appreciation of serious music, but, above all, the general standards of the orchestras and choruses. It is only natural that he was very critical of the bad performances, but he was also the first to applaud many impressive productions—impressive by their thoroughness of preparation and precise execution.

Whether he ever admitted it or not, he had had a unique

opportunity for improving his own conducting technique. No years of leading an able ensemble could have given him the experience he acquired by working with poor orchestras. And he had had too many disappointments not to become less critical of human frailties and more tolerant in his dealings with musicians.

Berlioz planned next to go to Leipzig where Mendelssohn reigned supreme, although he hesitated until he received a letter from Mendelssohn cordially inviting him. He arrived in Leipzig just in time to attend a rehearsal Mendelssohn was conducting of his latest work—the *Walpurgisnacht*. He was amazed at the exactitude and spirit of the orchestra and the beautiful voices in the chorus, and, of course, by the composition itself, which he thought was Mendelssohn's finest to date. He had not yet heard Mendelssohn's A *Midsummer Night's Dream* overture.

Genuinely entranced, Berlioz went up to the composer as soon as he finished conducting.

"And is it really twelve years? Twelve years since we dreamed together on the plains of Rome?" Mendelssohn asked.

The exchange of reminiscences continued, and then Berlioz said, "I am going to ask you to make me a present, to which I shall attach the greatest value."

"What is it?" Mendelssohn asked.

"Give me the baton with which you have just conducted the rehearsal of your new work."

"Oh . . . willingly, on condition that you send me yours."

"I shall be giving copper for gold," was Berlioz's gallant way of closing the bargain.

Next day Berlioz sent word of thanks to the composer: "Great chief! We have promised to exchange tomahawks. Mine is a rough one—yours is plain. Only squaws and pale-faces are fond of ornate weapons. Be my brother! and when the Great Spirit sends us to hunt in the land of souls, may

The concert hall of the Gewandhaus in Leipzig

our warriors hang up our tomahawks together at the door of the council chamber."

Throughout Hector's life Mendelssohn's baton remained one of the few mementos he cherished.

"When it came to organizing my concerts Mendelssohn really did treat me like a brother," Berlioz wrote in his *Mémoires*. Indeed no other of his musician contemporaries had taken so much time and given so much attention and energy as did Mendelssohn in helping Berlioz prepare the *Romeo and Juliet* for his Leipzig program. He revised the faulty German translation of the text and rehearsed the chorus, he procured the instruments unavailable in Leipzig, and he himself even played on the piano the harpist's part in the score.

It was a new and great experience for Berlioz to conduct the Gewandhaus Orchestra in this long program which, in addition to *Romeo and Juliet*, had his *King Lear* and *Les Francs-Juges* overtures as well as the *Symphonie fantastique*. The ensemble, well trained by Mendelssohn, delighted Berlioz by its courtesy and perfect response to all his demands, and the two concerts Berlioz gave in Leipzig during February,

1843, had exceptional success. Even Marie's participation in both performances, politely indulged by her listeners, did not mar the general impression made by Berlioz's works.

The three weeks between the two Leipzig concerts Berlioz spent in Dresden, where he met the thirty-year-old Richard Wagner. Having heard of the difficulties the young composer had encountered in his own country at the beginning of his career, and of his fruitless struggle to establish himself in Paris, Berlioz was happy to see Wagner now at the helm of the Dresden Orchestra as an associate conductor. He also had the opportunity of hearing *Rienzi* and *The Flying Dutchman*, the two operas whose success had gained Wagner his appointment to his post by the King of Saxony. Because Berlioz had only once heard some parts of the operas, his opinion of them had included some reservations, which nevertheless had not limited his admiration for Wagner's talent.

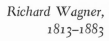

Richard Wagner,
1813–1883

Probably because he was still intoxicated by his newly acquired position, Wagner was—for Richard Wagner—exceptionally courteous and helpful to his French guest. He was very cooperative at Berlioz's rehearsals with the orchestra, which Berlioz found almost as good as that in Leipzig, thanks to Wagner's endeavors to keep alive the traditional discipline imbued by Weber, who had led the ensemble for many years in the past.

Always a great admirer of Weber's works, Berlioz later regretted that no one had told him about the composer's widow and children living in Dresden. As a student in Paris, Hector had missed meeting Weber, and now he missed the opportunity of paying his respects to Weber's family.

The two concerts in Dresden were so successful that Berlioz was able to send some five hundred francs to Harriet and, added to his most pleasant sojourn in Leipzig, it put him in a more cheerful frame of mind for the rest of his tour. He concertized in a number of large cities—Hamburg, Hanover, Brunswick, Darmstadt, and Berlin—as well as in several smaller towns. He found appreciative audiences in some of these, but in the others his music was too new, too strange to be understood.

By the end of April he was too weary to go to Breslau, Munich, and Vienna. He was restless because he was inwardly drawn to Paris where, he felt, music was at once sublime and commonplace, "lofty and mean, a beggar and king, exalted and despised, adored and insulted."

Toward the end of May, 1843, Marie and Hector returned to Paris.

*Chapter
Eleven*

*B*erlioz was in Paris barely a few days when he realized that his situation, domestic and artistic, far from having improved, had become more acute. He had to face the inevitable —he could not continue living with Harriet, even on the part-time basis they had effected. He was not only depressed by her appearance, which she was neglecting more and more, but by the spectacle of the slovenly conditions in which their son was being reared. Yet he had no intention of deserting his family. He remained its sole financial support, and by frequent visits he kept up the appearances of a friendly relationship. But he moved into Marie's apartment, where with her mother Marie made him a "second" home as best she could.

No longer because of Marie's artistic ambitions, but simply to lessen the strain on his finances from keeping two establishments, Berlioz secured Marie an engagement at the Opéra-Comique. Her debut on August 18, 1843, however, was such a failure that even Hector's influence with the critics could not save her reputation. Marie had to resign herself to simply being useful to him at home, but she objected to her position as Berlioz's mistress and often became a burden in his social life.

She resented Harriet who, she thought, was the sole obstacle to her legalizing her relationship with Hector, and who drained their finances. She hated her so much that one day she appeared on the doorstep of Harriet's apartment, dressed for the occasion in her best to show Harriet what a pretty and elegant young woman she was. Harriet opened the door, and, having never seen her before, asked Marie whom she wished to see.

Smiling, Marie said: "I want to see Madame Berlioz."

"I am she," Harriet replied.

"You are wrong," Marie said. "You are talking about the old Madame Berlioz, the discarded one. *I* mean the young one, the pretty one, the one he prefers. Well, *that* one is myself." And she slammed the door in Harriet's face and walked away.

When the friend to whom Hector confessed this unattractive side of Marie's character asked him why he did not leave her, all that Berlioz could say was: "How could I? I love her."

Indeed he must have loved her, but he would have preferred to be spared the description of the vulgar scene, which made him suffer for Harriet who, insulted by Marie, had almost fainted in her misery. He loved Marie as he had loved Camille. Neither Camille nor Marie ever symbolized his "Estella montis," which Harriet had done, if only at the beginning of their romance. His *idée fixe*, not effaced by the passing years, colored his feelings toward these women, who in his mind could never approach his ideal.

Such a state of affairs in his personal life was hardly likely to assuage his depression, caused also by his realization that his reports from Germany had not had the anticipated effect on his reputation and popularity in Paris. Quite the contrary: far from being in demand, Berlioz now again had to make

A caricature of
Hector Berlioz

Er. CARJAT.

ends meet, supplementing his meager salary of about one hundred and twenty-five francs a month as a librarian at the Conservatory by regularly writing criticisms and *feuilletons*—stories and articles which had no relation to music—for one hundred francs each.

Although he had developed into a brilliant writer, he abhorred writing the *feuilletons* because, as he said, he did not always care to express opinions on the subjects he was forced to write about. And yet, whatever the topic, he had to leave the impression of being for or against it. It required an intricate technique of writing which did not, as he said, "amuse" him. And as for the regular musical reviews, they were just as repulsive to him because he hated to be forced either to lick somebody's boots or bite his head off.

"Oh, let me have scores to write, orchestras to conduct, rehearsals to direct," Berlioz cried in desperation. "Let me stand eight or ten hours at a time, baton in hand, training choruses without accompaniment, singing their refrain myself, and beating time till I spit blood and till my arms are paralyzed with cramps; let me carry desks, double basses, harps, let me nail planks like a carpenter, and, by way of rest, let me correct proofs or copies at night. All this I have done, I do, I will do. It is part of my life as a musician, and I can bear it without a murmur or even a thought, as the sportsman endures cold, heat, hunger, thirst, sun, rain, dust, and the thousand fatigues of the game.

"But everlastingly to have to write *feuilletons* for one's bread, to write nothing about nothing, to speak one day of a great master and the next of an idiot with the same seriousness, in the same language; to employ one's time, intelligence, courage, and patience, all the while knowing that not even then will one be able to serve art by destroying a few abuses, removing prejudices, enlightening opinions, purifying the public taste, or putting men and things in their proper order and place—this indeed is the lowest depth of degradation! Better to be finance minister in a republic . . . had I but the chance!"

To break out of the monotony of his literary profession, Berlioz was glad to accept an assignment from Léon Pillet, now the director of the Opéra. Pillet was planning to produce Weber's *Der Freischütz,* and he asked Hector to transform into recitative the spoken prose dialogues that were inter-

"Two hands for one arm" (*Cartoon by Grandville*)

spersed with the different arias and choruses of the opera. But by the time the opera went into production, so many liberties had been taken with the score—cuts, as well as insertions of other music into Weber's work—that aside from being credited with the recitatives and the orchestration of Weber's piano piece *Invitation à la valse* (for the accompaniment of the ballet) Berlioz did not want to have his name connected with the production.

Despite the usual struggle of assembling a capable orchestra, finding a suitable hall and, above all, obtaining the finances, Berlioz gave two successful concerts on November 19, 1843, and on February 3, 1844. At the second of these he introduced for the first time *Le Carnaval romain* overture which he had composed during January, 1844.

Once again the memories of his sojourn in Rome must have influenced him—*influenced* rather than inspired, if the latter word is taken at its true meaning, which connotes exaltation. For Berlioz hated everything connected with carnivals, whether in Rome or Paris, where they were called *les jours gras*. "Fat days, indeed!" Berlioz shuddered. "Fat with grease, ointment, and paint, stale wine, coarse jokes, and prostitutes, drunken detectives, vile masks, worn-out hacks, laughing fools, gaping idiots, and weary idlers."

In Paris they still adhered to the old custom of parading the Fat Bull for three days during the carnival, after which he was slain with great pomp, to the delight of the delirious spectators. "In Rome," according to Berlioz, "where the good old tradition of the past still survived, a human sacrifice was offered up during the carnival. In those days some poor devil under sentence of death was retained for this purpose; he, too, was fattened, so as to be worthy of the god—the Roman people—to whom he was to be sacrificed. . . . When the hour struck, this rabble of fools from all nations, this horde of well-dressed savages, weary of watching the races, of pelting each

Carnival in Paris: the parading of the Fat Bull

other with plaster sweetmeats, and laughing at the refinement of their own wit, adjourned to see the man die."

But even the fair success of his latest work did not affect Berlioz's melancholy, which he ascribed to "a certain uneasiness, a vague suffering of the heart, an objective sorrow, causeless regrets, ardent aspirations toward the unknown, and an inexpressible restlessness of the whole being." The truth of the matter was that Berlioz was suffering from inactivity—a condition not congenial to his energetic and passionate nature.

He missed the turbulent but exciting artistic life he had been leading during the many months of his tour in Germany; he felt about his present success as if it were the day after a great celebration given in his honor by strangers. Above all he missed the splendid orchestras and choruses with which he had had opportunity to work, as well as the courteous and enthusiastic audiences, unprejudiced against the venturesome essays of modern art. It all was like a drug to him, and he longed for it.

With his unused energy he enthusiastically threw himself into a typical Berliozian enterprise—a grandiose three-day festival consisting of a concert, a ball, and a banquet for the participants at the Paris Industrial Exhibition (1844), which was

about to close. The functions were to take place on the premises of the exhibition, thus involving Berlioz in intricate arguments with the prefect of the police and the minister of the interior in order to obtain the necessary permissions. To this, of course, were added the usual difficulties of organizing several orchestras, choruses, and soloists, including a band to accompany the dancing—in all a body of over one thousand performers.

The well-advertised *fête* brought thirty-two thousand francs in receipts, eight hundred francs of profits, and left Berlioz wholly exhausted. Upon his doctor's urgent orders he went to Nice to recuperate.

After a few weeks there he recovered sufficiently to give two concerts in Marseilles and two in Lyons in June and July, and to attend the inauguration of the Beethoven memorial at Bonn in August—a project which had been realized thanks to Franz Liszt's generous financial contribution as well as his personal participation in the event.

Whether or not it was due to the influence of Liszt, who had given up Paris in preference for concertizing in central Europe, Berlioz decided also to escape what he called a stagnant situation in Paris by continuing his concert tour, which he had interrupted two years before. On October 22, 1845, accompanied by Marie, he went to Vienna.

Chapter
Twelve

*B*ut no matter to what extent concert tours had become part of his life, and no matter how much the intoxication of success was almost necessary for his well-being, Berlioz did not give up composing. Shortly after his return from Bonn, and again most probably influenced by Liszt, who was a great admirer of Goethe's work, Berlioz started on what he planned to be an opera—*The Damnation of Faust.*

He wrote the score with a facility he had rarely experienced in his other compositions—the ideas, as he said, presenting themselves in the most unforeseen order. He continued to work during this second journey abroad—in the stagecoaches, on steamboats, and in hotels, whenever he found time between rehearsals and concerts.

His tour took him to Vienna, Budapest, Prague, and Breslau, and it was as triumphant artistically as it was pleasant socially. His concerts were enthusiastically acclaimed and he was feted by the nobility as well as by the common folk.

In Budapest he was almost prevented from introducing his own quickly written version of the *Rákóczy March* (a popular

Hungarian tune), because at the beginning of the composition he had the main theme announced *piano* by flutes and clarinets. The Hungarians expected the usual loud statement of the melody. "Be patient," Berlioz advised; "it is the *end* that counts in everything." And indeed who but Berlioz could bring the final climax of the composition to such a roof-raising tonal volume as to make even the Hungarian audience delirious.

Its obvious effect led Berlioz to use the *Rákóczy March* in his *Faust*. Later he was severely criticized by the German critics for taking such liberties as to place Dr. Faust in Hungary and make him a witness at the march of the Hungarian army across the plain. But Hector, who in writing the libretto did not faithfully follow Goethe's text any more than he had followed Shakespeare's when he composed his *Romeo and Juliet*, saw no reason why he should not let his hero travel anywhere, as long as it benefited the score. The German criticisms, however, did not come until years later, and therefore had no effect on Berlioz's own triumphant march on his tour.

In fact Berlioz had become so used to ovations in Vienna, Budapest, and Prague that he felt uncomfortable when in Breslau he encountered the peculiar tradition by which audiences, when deeply moved, refrained from applauding to show their respect for a composition. Berlioz was sincerely afraid of being "respected," for he had learned well from bitter experience that an audience is a sea always more or less rough, but its dead calm is more terrifying to artists than its tempests.

Upon his return to Paris early in May, 1846, he occupied himself with putting together the already sketched parts of *Faust*, as well as with orchestrating the score, which so far had only indications here and there for the instruments. *The Damnation of Faust* was completed on October 19, 1846, thus launching Berlioz on the familiar wearisome road of trying to get for it a public performance.

Except for its smaller dimensions, *The Damnation of Faust*

LA
Damnation
DE
FAUST
PAR
HECTOR
BERLIOZ

was what Berlioz called a "concert–opera"—an opera in concert form. Remembering the eager attitude of the public when *Romeo and Juliet* had first been announced, Berlioz believed that now—even more so as his name had gained in prestige as a result of his success abroad—he was justified in risking considerable expense for the performance.

He rented the Opéra-Comique and assembled a good orchestra and chorus, but unfortunately was unable to engage the singers who were in vogue at that time in Paris for the principal roles of Dr. Faust and Marguerite, thus missing out on a valuable asset to the box office. As fate would have it, even the weather was against him. It was snowing on the day of the first performance, December 6, 1846; the hall was half empty. The composition failed to produce the effect he had hoped for, and the repeat performance on December 20 was attended by an even smaller audience.

"Nothing in all my artistic career ever wounded me so deeply as this unexpected indifference from the Parisian public," Berlioz wrote in his *Mémoires*. He had gotten himself into debt with no visible prospect of repayment, and now he could no longer hope to obtain the permanent post of conductor at the Opéra, which might have rescued him from the hated journalistic work. Berlioz was completely ruined financially.

As a way out of his predicament, Berlioz decided to try his luck in Russia, which at that time was considered a veritable gold mine for visiting European artists. He needed a large sum for this enterprise. And yet as soon as the news of his intentions had spread in Paris, he discovered that the money was more easily available for this plan than for any of his previous projects. Thousands of francs were offered him not only by his friends, but also by complete strangers, and

A poster advertising a performance of The Damnation of Faust

Honoré de Balzac, the French novelist, who had just returned
from Russia, assured Berlioz of making a fortune there.

Berlioz gladly accepted Balzac's offer of a fur coat, but as
for his enthusiastic prediction, Hector was more encouraged
by Franz Liszt's experiences during his concert tour in Russia.
Liszt did earn large sums from his concerts there. His real
fortune, however, as Berlioz later learned, came from Princess
Wittgenstein, a rich young woman whom Liszt had met there
and who bound her life and wealth with his.

The three-month visit in Saint Petersburg and Moscow
from mid-February to the end of May did more than gratify
Berlioz's well-wishers and his own hopes. The enthusiasm
with which he was welcomed grew in intensity with each of
Hector's public appearances. His concert programs included
the *Roman Carnival,* the first two parts of *Faust,* and *Romeo
and Juliet.*

If the Russians could not provide Berlioz with orchestras
of such excellent quality as those he had had the pleasure of
conducting in Germany, they certainly showed no lack of
fervor in working with him. When he asked how many re-
hearsals he could have, he was told as many as he needed to
be satisfied—a comment almost as pleasant as were the re-
sults of his performances. He received ovations, demands for
encores, and was showered with flowers. But above all, the
receipts from his first concert in Saint Petersburg brought
eighteen thousand francs, which minus expenses left Berlioz
with a clear profit of twelve thousand francs. "I am saved,"
Berlioz thought. His second concert two weeks later brought
him another eight thousand francs. "I am a rich man!" Berlioz
exclaimed. Unfortunately, Marie was not there to enjoy the
windfall with him—she had been left behind at the outset
precisely because of Hector's sorry finances.

As music in Russia during the last century was mainly enjoyed by the nobility and the rich, Berlioz was given a taste of this life at sumptuous banquets held in his honor and at the special performances he had an opportunity of witnessing. But despite, or perhaps because of his overwhelming emotions at the time, he suddenly suffered one of his fits of depression.

It happened to him after the second performance of *Romeo and Juliet* in Saint Petersburg. The performance was so close to perfection that it was to remain in his memory as one of the greatest delights of his life. The theater was packed to the last seat—uniforms, epaulettes, helmets, and diamonds glittered on all sides. "I don't remember how often I was called back," Berlioz said, "but I confess I didn't pay much attention to the public. And such was the impression made upon me by that divine Shakespearean poem as I sang it to myself that, after the finale, I fled for refuge into one of the side rooms where I cried like a hysterical girl for a good quarter of an hour." His mind was assailed by memories of his youth, of Estelle, his first love, and of Harriet's "Juliet."

Berlioz needed at his side someone whom he loved and who loved him. He needed to share with her his happiness and to share another kind of love, the kind he felt was true, poetic love: "the love of art." He had known this since the first time he had fallen in love and nothing was more beautiful to him. "The love of art," he had often said; "there is no other divinity of the human heart. With it the world grows bright, horizons enlarge, all nature takes on color and vibrates in endless harmonies, and—one loves, that's all, one loves!"

But was there anyone, not merely imaginary like his Estelle, or "Juliet," who could fill this place? It was said in Saint Petersburg that while there he was attracted to a young Russian woman who sang in his chorus. She was a corset-maker, engaged to a man who was temporarily in Sweden. Berlioz had been seen taking walks with her at sunset on the banks of the Neva. "I crushed her arm against my breast," he later confessed to a friend, "and I sang to her the melody of the adagio in *Romeo and Juliet*," since the young woman's limited French had made conversation difficult.

Was she another "Estella montis," "ever dreamt of, ever sought for, and never attained?" Or was she merely his Gretchen—just another naïve, innocent girl?

That it was not a passing fancy can be presumed from his letters to a friend in Saint Petersburg, written six months and again nine months after his departure from Russia. Not having heard from the young woman—her letters having failed to reach him—Berlioz enclosed a letter for her in one to his friend, asking his friend to deliver it personally. Eventually she wrote Berlioz that her fiancé had returned from Sweden and that she would always remain grateful to Berlioz for his affection. Six months later, during the summer of 1848, Berlioz was to put the final touch to this episode by completing two compositions: *La Mort d'Ophélie* (*Death of Ophelia*), for female chorus and orchestra, and the *Marche funèbre* [*Funeral March*] *pour la dernière scène d'Hamlet*.

Sad news was awaiting him in Paris. Harriet's health was steadily deteriorating: she had suffered a stroke which had impaired her speech. His sister Nanci was ill with cancer of the breast, and his father, now old and ailing, was alone at La Côte-Saint-André. Berlioz had not seen his seventy-one-year-old father for fifteen years, nor had Louis, his twelve-year-old boy, ever met his grandparents. In the middle of September, Berlioz took his son to La Côte-Saint-André, and for two weeks he gave himself up completely to enjoying his old home, run by the same old servants, and to his family and their friends.

Dr. Berlioz was suffering from gastritis and was growing deaf, but this did not prevent him from being entertained

Easter week in nineteenth-century Saint Petersburg

by his son's stories. He, who had been so much against Hector's persistence in becoming a musician, now took great pride in his accomplishments and would make him describe them over and over again. His favorite story was about the postmaster at Tilsit whom Hector had met on his way to Russia.

" 'Are you Monsieur Nernst?' I asked," Hector recounted to his father. " 'Yes, sir,' he replied, and asked me who I was. 'I am Hector Berlioz,' I said. 'What! Nothing else!' he exclaimed."

"Ha, ha. . . . 'Nothing else!' *Rien que çà!*" Dr. Berlioz chuckled. "And you say it happened in Tilsit?"

"Yes, at the extreme frontier of Prussia," Hector explained.

"In Prussia!" Dr. Berlioz repeated, very much impressed by his son's world fame. "Ha, ha. . . . *Rien que çà!*" Dr. Berlioz kept on repeating, laughing with pleasure.

He said to Hector that his greatest desire was to hear his

Requiem. "I would like to hear that terrible *Dies Irae*, of which they talk so much. Then . . . I would gladly say my *Nunc dimittis.*" But Dr. Berlioz never heard a single note of his son's music. He died the following year, on July 28, 1848.

Dr. Berlioz had been sorry to learn of his son's tragic matrimonial situation, but was delighted to see his delicate and pale grandson. Hector did everything he could to make his boy's first vacation in the country so pleasant that years later Louis wrote to him that those two weeks at La Côte-Saint-André remained unforgettable ones for him. As if he were an older brother, Hector joined in his son's games, or took him on long hiking trips in the mountains.

But this carefree life had to come to an end, as Berlioz had accepted an engagement to conduct several concerts in London. On his way to England he left Louis at a boarding school in Rouen, for living with his mother was made impossible by Harriet's disastrous condition. Hector often spoke to Louis about what profession he might choose, but the boy's sole desire was to travel, and indeed he eventually became an officer in the French Merchant Marine.

Despite his success in Russia, Hector's financial state was again such that he could not afford to take Marie with him to London. Once there, his situation became even shakier. His first visit to England was a dismal failure. According to his contract, Berlioz was to receive four hundred pounds for a month's concerts, in addition to eight hundred pounds for composing an opera in three acts. He should have known better than to get involved with Louis Antoine Jullien, with whom he signed this lucrative contract.

The thirty-six-year-old Jullien, who ten years before had escaped to London from his creditors in Paris, had for a while made himself well known in London as a conductor by exploiting his showmanship. In a coat thrown wide open, white waistcoat, and elaborately embroidered shirt, he waved his baton with gravity and magnificence, reported *Punch* Magazine. All Beethoven's symphonies were conducted with a jeweled baton and in a pair of white kid gloves, handed him on a silver salver. The climax of certain compositions brought him to such ecstasy that he could not refrain from seizing a violin or piccolo to heighten the impression on the audience. But shortly after Berlioz arrived in London at the beginning of November, Jullien was headed for bankruptcy.

For two concerts of his own works, which Berlioz conducted in February, 1848, he did not receive a penny—the black-haired, black-moustached manager had pocketed the receipts himself. Then, with the French Revolution of 1848, came the downfall of the monarchy, threatening the abolishment of the *Journal des Débats*, the periodical for which Berlioz was writing, and of his librarian's post at the Conservatory—his only other sources of income. Berlioz could not have been in worse financial straits when Marie suddenly arrived in London.

Because of some misunderstanding, Hector's promissory notes, which he signed before going to London, had been presented for payment at Marie's address. Marie referred the money-collector to Harriet, his legal wife, at Hector's legal residence. Violent scenes ensued between the two women. The quarrel ended by Marie's mother taking other lodgings, while Marie hastened to London to complain to Hector.

Berlioz gave one more concert at the end of June, but with no financial profit worth mentioning. Gustave Roger, a French tenor visiting London at the time, had this to say: "Berlioz is an eagle who dwells on peaks, in the clouds; but that is not where gold mines are found."

After this last unrewarding enterprise, his bankrupt manager preferred to disappear, leaving Hector with no other alternative than to return to Paris.

With most of the musicians, writers, and artists absent

from Paris during the revolution, the city was in a mournful state as far as art was concerned. Hector's periodical had survived, and although he was now receiving only half of his former fee per article, still he was fortunate to have this additional income to add to his salary as librarian at the Conservatory—a post which even for the sake of economy the new Republic did not deem necessary to abolish. But this was not sufficient to keep Harriet and Louis, Marie and her mother, and himself alive.

He was forced to incur new debts. To add to his distress he learned from his sisters at La Côte-Saint-André of his father's death. As they had not known where to reach him, he received the sad news only after it was too late for him to be present at his father's last hours, but three weeks later, as soon as he had managed to settle his most pressing financial problems and had pacified Harriet and Marie, he went down to La Côte-Saint-André to be with his grieving sisters.

Hector's share of the estate left by his father amounted to some one hundred and thirty thousand francs, a considerable sum which would have relieved his financial crisis, but due to the political situation in France it would take years before Hector could have access to it.

As might have been expected, the death of his father and the reunion with his sisters evoked in him reminiscences of his youth and of their lives together in the parental home.

"With a strange thirst for sorrow I longed to see again the scene of my first passionate emotions," Berlioz wrote in his *Mémoires*. "I wished to embrace my whole past, to intoxicate myself with recollections, however harrowing they might be."

His sisters, aware of his intention of visiting Meylan, where his Estelle used to live, discreetly stayed behind and let him go alone on this "sacred pilgrimage." "I feel my heart beat at the notion of relating this excursion," Berlioz wrote in his *Mémoires*. "But I will do it, if it be but to prove the persistency of old feelings, so irreconcilable with the new, and the reality of their coexistence in a heart which forgets nothing."

As if to savor to the full the object of his visit, he prolonged the excursion to Estelle's house by first going to his grandfather's home. Since his grandfather's death the new proprietor of the house had not yet moved in. There was no one in the house, and Hector moved slowly from one room to another examining every piece of furniture and every object on the walls and tables. Everything seemed to him as when he had seen it for the last time thirty-two years before. He walked into the drawing room, but when it reminded him of his Estelle dancing there with his uncle, he rushed out.

He walked through the orchard, which was plowed, hoping to find there the bench on which his father used to sit in the evenings, wrapped in his own thoughts. Only two worm-eaten wooden legs of the bench remained. And he saw the cornfield where he used to hide with the first sorrows of his unhappy love.

It was a warm autumn day, full of poetic charm and serenity, which, added to his anticipation of seeing Estelle's home, made his heart beat faster as he went up the road toward the mountain. He thought that he had recognized the alley of trees, but it ended in a vineyard. He had lost his way.

He walked to a farm near-by and "trembling like a thief pursued by the police," asked the way to the "white villa" which used to belong to Madame Gautier, Estelle's grandmother. At first no one seemed to know the name, but Hector persisted until an old woman, who had overheard his inquiries from the farmhouse doorway, said: "Oh yes, an old lady . . . of course I remember Mademoiselle Estelle—she was so pretty that everyone used to stop at the church door on Sundays to see her pass."

Berlioz followed the path the old woman had indicated. Now, he felt, just behind that little fountain that he heard

*Hector Berlioz
(Photograph from
about 1850)*

murmuring, he would see Estelle. He passed the gate to the
garden, where a man in city clothes was lighting his pipe.
Probably the new owner of the white villa, Berlioz thought.
The man looked at him with amazement, but did not say
a word, and Hector, instead of going toward the house, went
up the hill to the tower where he had once sat with his father
and where he had played for him on his flute one of his first
compositions.

There he remained for a while admiring the view of the
valley below, the Alps, the glaciers, the rock of Saint Eynard
—the view which Estelle had admired. He saw himself as a
twelve-year-old boy walking on the cliff when she called to
him: "Take care! Don't go so near the edge!" Berlioz would
have given anything to hear those words again. He fell on
his knees, crying aloud: "Estelle! Estelle!" But only an echo
in the mountains answered his call.

Like a lost dog in search of his master, he looked for a
small rock where "her lovely feet once rested," where he had
seen her graceful figure standing and admiring the view. That
day he had said to himself: "When I grow up, and have be-
come a famous composer, I will write an opera on Florian's
Estelle. I will dedicate it to her, and bring the score to this

very rock, where she shall find it some morning when she comes to see the sun rise."

But the rock was no longer there. The mountain winds must have buried it in the sand, Berlioz thought, as he slowly descended again to the village.

Still dazed by his experience he went to the hamlet of Murianette, where he called on his cousins and their mother. On the following day he returned with them to Grenoble.

"What's the matter with you? I have never seen you like this before," Victor, his cousin, asked him when they were alone. Berlioz told him about his excursion to Meylan. "Oh, Madame Fornier?" Victor said. "The one they used to call the beautiful Estelle Duboeuf? But she must be now over fifty years old. Her eldest son must be twenty-two; we went through our law course together."

He told Berlioz that she had had six children, that her two daughters had died, and that since the death of her husband she had been living with her four sons at Vif.

Vif was only ten miles from Grenoble and Berlioz wanted to go there immediately. His cousin advised against this visit, particularly because of his emotional state. "You will only make a fool of yourself and compromise her, that's all," Victor said. "Wouldn't it be better to keep your youthful memories and preserve your ideal?"

Finally, instead of visiting her, Hector wrote her a letter:

"Madame,

"There are certain persistent memories that only die when we die. . . . I was twelve years old when I saw Mademoiselle Estelle for the first time at Meylan. You could not have known how you overwhelmed my childish heart, ready to break beneath the burden of its feelings. I believe that you were even so cruel as to laugh at me.

"Seventeen years later, on my return from Italy, my eyes

filled with tears—the silent tears of memory—when I entered
our valley and caught sight of the house where you once lived,
on the romantic heights overlooking Saint Eynard. Some days
afterward, before I knew your married name, I was asked to
deliver a letter addressed to Madame Fornier. I waited for her
at one of the station-stops of the stagecoach by which she was
traveling. I presented her with the letter; a violent stab at my
heart made my hand tremble as it approached hers. I recog-
nized the object of my admiration, the 'Estella montis' whose
radiant beauty illuminated the morning of my life.

"Yesterday, madame, after far distant travels through Eu-
rope, after labors, an echo of which may perhaps have reached
you, I undertook with violent agitation the long contemplated
pilgrimage. Once more I desired to see everything, and I have
done so—the white villa, the garden, the hill, the old tower,
the everlasting rock of Saint Eynard, and the sublime scenery
so worthy of your admiration. Nothing has changed. Time
has respected the temple of my memory. But strangers inhabit
it now; your flowers are tended by other hands, and no one,
not even yourself, could have guessed why a saddened man,
with features furrowed by labor and sorrow, should have pene-
trated to its most secret recesses. *O quánte lagrime!*

"Farewell, madame, I must return to the whirlwind of my
life. You will probably never see me, never know who I am;
and I hope you will pardon the strange liberty I am now taking
in writing to you. I forgive you if you smile at the recollections
of the man, as you laughed at the admiration of the child."

Berlioz signed the letter not with his name, but with "De-
spised Love," a quotation from *Hamlet*.

He planned to return to Grenoble in a few months, and
then he would go to see Estelle. But he never learned what
befell the letter he mailed her, and the "whirlwind of his life"
intervened before he ever reached Grenoble.

Part Three

Chapter Thirteen

*I*n Paris Hector found Harriet a helpless invalid. She was paralyzed, unable either to move or speak coherently. During the following six years she was a living corpse; she needed two nurses and almost daily doctor's visits. Hector spent many nights by her bedside. Once, when from pure exhaustion he fell asleep, he dreamed so vividly about a symphony he was going to compose that on awakening he remembered the whole first movement—an allegro in two/four time—and even the key, A minor.

He was going to write down immediately what he had "heard" in his dream, but on second thought he gave it up. Pictures of the everlasting struggle—the humiliation and distress he had encountered with all his previous compositions in Paris—assailed his tired mind, and Harriet's groans from the adjoining room crippled his energy. The dream reappeared on the following day and this time he not only distinctly heard the symphony, but could see it written down. The next morning he could hum the major themes, but he stoically hardened himself against the temptation. The symphony was never written, nor could he force himself at the time to compose anything else.

An additional misfortune next befell his wearied mind. His sister Nanci died of cancer in Grenoble on May 4, 1850, and his sister Adèle, who remained at her bedside during the last six months of her suffering, nearly succumbed herself.

Hector had not yet reached his fiftieth birthday, but he was already an old man. He was resigned to his life—to the emotional vortex in which he lived, to the labor, and to the sorrow to which he felt destined. He expected none of this to change. Nor did he expect anything from his Parisian public; but he could not go on an extensive concert tour as he had done before and leave Harriet with no one besides a nurse to look after her. Harriet's mother and sister had died, and if she had any relatives in Ireland she no longer had any connection with them.

And yet, just when everything was appearing so gloomy, Berlioz was invited to assume the leadership of the recently founded New Philharmonic Society in London. Accompanied by Marie he arrived in London at the end of February, 1852.

Belgrave Square in London

At his third concert in March Madame Camille Pleyel, his former fiancée, was the soloist in Weber's *Concertstück*. It remains unknown as to how pleasant or unpleasant Berlioz found this surprise, and just how he felt about having Camille, whom he had once planned to murder, now participating in his performance. Unlike Marie, Camille was a brilliant artist, but while she claimed that Berlioz had failed to do justice to her pianistic qualities in his orchestral accompaniment, Berlioz, for his part, must have been indifferent to this professional encounter, for he never spoke about it. He was far more concerned with the financial profits his concerts were reaping and with their public success, which not only led to return engagements but could have established him in a permanent post as conductor of the Society had his limited knowledge of the English language not been a considerable handicap.

Upon his return to Paris Berlioz received some pleasant news. Liszt, who since 1848 had given up concertizing and had settled in Weimar, where he had become the sole master of all the musical activities of that city, invited Berlioz to attend a "Berlioz Week" he had organized in his honor. In addition to this Liszt had arranged for performances of Berlioz's opera *Benvenuto Cellini*.

Overjoyed by the turn in his fortunes, Berlioz took the opportunity of his presence in Germany to give a number of concerts in many cities where he had already made himself known. The proprietor of the Casino at Baden-Baden had become such an admirer that he offered Berlioz carte blanche —a complete free hand—in choosing his own programs for a practically unlimited number of performances during the annual summer festival.

At last, Berlioz hoped, his popularity abroad would change the attitude of the Parisian audiences; at last, he believed, he could abandon the journalistic drudgery. But it was not to be. The two books which he had published, *Voyage musical en Allemagne et en Italie* and *Les Soirées de l'orchestre*, were so well received, the critics praising his keen observation and wit, that Berlioz was mortified to realize that the Parisians still liked him better as a journalist than as a composer.

This distressing thought understandably affected his desire to compose. He had recently completed his *Te Deum* after five years of work and was awaiting its first public performance. Of his oratorio *L'Enfance du Christ* he had managed so far to introduce only the second part—the *Fuite en Egypte*—at one of his concerts in London. He was too discouraged to start another major work whose unfortunate fate he could easily predict.

He had reconciled himself to Harriet's condition, but his son, Louis, now contributed new worries. The young man suddenly announced his desire to give up the sea. He did not know what to do with himself and was frivolously spending his own money as well as the money with which Hector felt obliged to assist him. Louis was an additional burden to his father until he was persuaded to return to his post in the Merchant Marine.

By the end of February, 1854, Harriet's suffering showed she was approaching the end of her life. Louis obtained a leave to join his father at her bedside, but he had to return to his ship at Cherbourg before she died on March 3 and could not be at her funeral, which was attended by only a few of his father's intimate friends.

Harriet Smithson, who as Ophelia and Juliet had held Parisian audiences breathless, was completely forgotten. She was buried in a little cemetery in Montmartre on the slope of a hill—her face turned toward the England she had never wished to see again.

Although he had been resigned to losing her for a long time, Hector was deeply moved by her death. In his grief he reviewed their life together, recalling the unfortunate turn in her career, and feeling again his gratitude to her for introducing him to Shakespeare's works, which had become the paramount inspiration of his own art. Analyzing his feelings for Harriet, his thoughts wandered to the peculiarities of his own character—he was, he said, often moved by a vague feeling of poetic love whenever he smelled a rose, or saw a harp. Estelle was the rose, and Harriet was the harp. "Alas," he sighed, "I have broken many of her strings."

Three weeks after Harriet's funeral, Marie and Hector went again on a concert tour to Germany. This time it was not an expedition filled with uncertainties such as he had described to Liszt several years before, but a venture assured of triumphs. He did not doubt that Germany would be a much happier ground for his artistic activities, but again, as in England, he would be denied a permanent conductor's post because of his inadequate knowledge of the language—a factor which would also prevent him from writing operas for the German stage. He was to remain what he already was—a most welcome guest conductor.

Marie was the only obstacle to Berlioz's complete satisfaction, with her incessant jealousy of other musicians, and particularly of Richard Wagner, whom she considered an unworthy rival to Hector. It caused an unfortunate "alienation of affections" toward Berlioz by that segment of the German public who were proud of their national composer. And it also caused unnecessary friction between the two musicians. But fortunately Marie had nothing against Franz Liszt.

During one of their summer visits to Weimar, Berlioz spoke at length with Liszt and Princess Wittgenstein, Liszt's consort and general adviser, about his long-cherished plan to write an opera on a grand scale. Their approval of his idea eventually gave birth to his writing *Les Troyens* (*The Trojans*). It took him three and one-half years to complete this opera, for

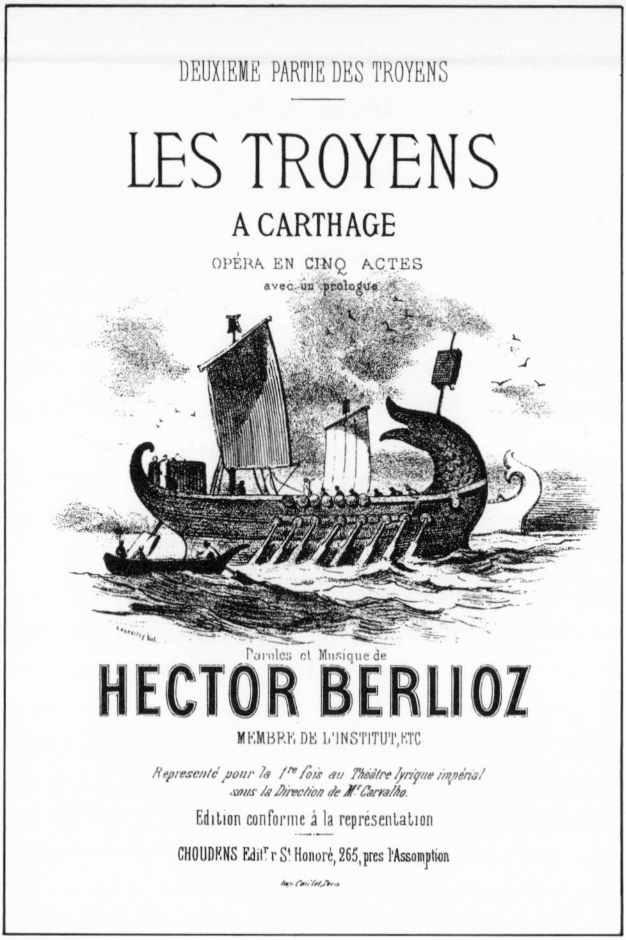

Title page from a score of Les Troyens à Carthage

which he himself wrote the poem. It consisted of two parts: "*La Prise de Troie*" (first and second acts), and "*Les Troyens à Carthage*" (third, fourth, and fifth acts).

Upon their return to Paris, on October 18, 1854, Berlioz married Marie. "My situation," he explained to his son, "is more fitting thus, being more regular." But Marie was not destined to see the production of *Les Troyens*. She had been suffering for years from a chronic heart condition, and on June 13, 1862, while she and Hector were spending the day with friends in the country near Paris, she died from a sudden heart attack. She was forty-eight years old.

Hector was very accustomed to the home Marie and her mother had provided him, and he preferred to remain in the care of this second mother-in-law, whom he promised never to forsake.

Was Marie's death the end of his romantic attachments? Not at all. It was not long before he met Amélie whose last name remains unknown. He made her acquaintance during one of his frequent visits to Marie's grave. The twenty-six-year-old Amélie, too, was visiting the grave of somebody close to her. They began to see each other often and even more often to correspond.

"Once more it was a matter of love—a love that came smiling to me, unsought by me, and that I fought against for a time," Berlioz later wrote to Humbert Ferrand, his lifelong friend. "But I was conquered by my loneliness and by the inexorable need for tenderness that was killing me. I let myself be loved, then I myself loved even more."

"But I am sixty!" Berlioz cried in desperation to a friend in whom he confided at the time of the romance. "Sometimes I sink into a chair and weep. The frightful thought assails me— she realizes it. And then with the tenderness of an angel she says to me: 'Oh, poor and unhappy man, how ungrateful you are. What can I do to convince you? Don't I risk a thousand dangers for you?' And she takes my head in her hands, and her tears fall on my neck. And yet, in spite of all this, always at the bottom of my heart I hear the dreadful words—'I am sixty! She cannot love me!' Ah, my friend, what torture to make one's own hell in a paradise!"

Finally, they agreed to separate completely and not to see or write to each other again. When they saw each other from a distance, a sign with the head was all that they exchanged. Amélie was already dying, but Hector was unaware of it. Six weeks later, in February, 1864, she was dead, but Berlioz did not learn of her death for another six months.

Chapter
Fourteen

" *I* am sixty-one," mused Hector Berlioz. "I have neither hopes, nor illusions, nor great ideas left. My son is nearly always absent. I am alone. My contempt for the folly and meanness of men, my hatred for their detestable ferocities nauseate me, and I hourly say to death: Whenever you are ready."

Indeed, the last years of his life brought him little joy from his art. The number of his enthusiastic followers was too small to have any decisive influence on his Parisian audiences, and the recognition abroad, contrary to his expectations, brought no change in his status. Although the frequent flattering news about performances of his works abroad still spurred his energy, he had lost his former verve for composing.

In the long lonely hours he reviewed his art, and no one was as good a critic as Berlioz himself. He realized that neither his intelligence and knowledge, nor his overwhelming energy and devotion to art, nor his extraordinary capacity for inspiring and commanding an orchestra, nor his clear vision of the purpose of dramatic compositions had a chance to overcome

the general trend of his compatriots' taste. They considered
him a madman because all music—including Beethoven's
Ninth Symphony—that deviated from the beaten track was,
in their opinion, the music of madmen. They preferred Meyer-
beer, Offenbach, and Gounod, and they accused Berlioz's
works of lacking melody. He agreed that the value of his mel-
odies, their distinction and charm, might be disputed, but the
failure of "hearing" them rested with the "lower stratum of
the musical world."

He believed that in his works he had clearly demonstrated
the predominant characteristics in his style: passionate expres-
sion and intense ardor, governed by dynamic rhythms.

He analyzed and tried to explain the critics' references to
his compositions as "architectural" works. "It is the form of
these pieces, the breadth of style, the progressions deliberately
prolonged toward goals not at once perceived, that give
these works their strange gigantic physiognomy and colossal
strength," he said.

But not all his works were written in this style. And yet,
even those that were conceived on an ordinary scale had failed
when not conducted by himself, because their expression and
rhythmical originality required "a combination of extreme pre-
cision and overwhelming verve, a regulated vehemence, a
dreamy tenderness, and an almost morbid melancholy," with-
out which the principal message of his work would be com-
pletely effaced. This is why he seldom enjoyed a performance
of his works by another conductor, except perhaps the favorite
of all his compositions—the love scene from *Romeo and Juliet*.
There the intense message of his music was too powerful to
be neglected.

But, he thought, even if he did not compose in a way the
public expected, it was against his grain to put up with slov-
enly performances. And to avoid these he had to be assured
of the good will and obedience of all the participants, espe-

cially in the lyric theater. Just as he "played on an orchestra," an opera to Berlioz was also an instrument, where he had to have complete control over everybody connected with it, from soloists and chorus down to scene-painters and stage-managers. Bitter experience convinced him that the intrigues and even conspiracies common to that world would have always prevented him from achieving his aim.

And now with his health deteriorating—he suffered from intestinal neuralgia—he had no strength to face the hostile criticism, even if he were offered all his required conditions.

Although as a conductor his supremacy was incontestable, he regretted that instead of friends, it brought him only jealous enemies among other conductors, to whom the orchestra men did not fail to show their preference for Berlioz. And finally his journalism, which he had pursued merely as a means of survival, had created an additional number of enemies, causing further obstacles to the production of his work and to his popularity.

Of the three books he had published so far he was proudest of the *Treatise of Instrumentation*, which to this day is still considered the standard theoretical work for every aspiring composer.

After Harriet's death in 1854 he had stopped writing his *Mémoires*, which he had begun in London in 1848. It is an extraordinary, but uneven, work. It shows him as the brilliant writer that he was, a keen observer and psychologist, witty, sarcastic, and at times belligerent. After eleven years of its having lain aside he was to write the final chapters—but not before the coda to his personal life had been played.

Berlioz was more than usually depressed in September, 1864, when most of his friends were away from Paris on their vacations, and after a short visit from Louis had left him feeling even lonelier than before. Suddenly a desire to see Madame Fornier, his Estelle, held him as if in a vise. For a pretext, as if he needed one, he decided to visit his nieces, Adèle's daughters, in Estressin, near Grenoble. There, through his brother-in-law, Adèle's husband, he was sure to find out whether Estelle was still alive and what was her address. Indeed she was alive, he was told, and was living in Lyons. But before pursuing his plan of calling on her, Berlioz made one more pilgrimage to Meylan, as if it were a necessary prelude to the sweet but imaginary love he had been tending all his life.

His excursion was an exact replica of his last visit there some sixteen years before. He lived through the same emotions, the

Hector Berlioz (Painting attributed to Daumier)

same craving for a "boundless affection." His "Estella montis" of the pink shoes had never left his mind.

Then he went to Lyons where, in feverish anticipation of the morrow, he spent a sleepless night. He planned to call on Madame Fornier at twelve o'clock, the conventional hour for a visit, but fearing that on hearing his name she might not wish to receive him, he wrote her a letter. He was too nervous to wait until midday. At eleven-thirty he was already ringing her doorbell. He gave the letter and his visiting card to the maid who opened the door and who automatically said: "Madame is not at home." But as he started down the stairs, he was called back by Madame Fornier, who was holding the unopened letter in her hand.

This was a great moment for Hector Berlioz, and it left him breathless. Some women succeed in retaining the beauty of their youth and can say, "time has touched me gently in his race." Madame Fornier was not so fortunate. However, in the stout, gray old lady dressed in black with a white bonnet tied under her chin, Berlioz perceived the dazzling loveliness of her past youth, the stateliness of her posture, and her charming smile.

"To me, fair friend, you never can be old,
    For as you were when first your eye I eye'd
    Such seems your beauty still,"
most certainly must have flashed through his mind.

"We are old acquaintances, Monsieur Berlioz," Madame Fornier calmly greeted him. "We were two children . . ."

"Please . . ." Hector stuttered, "please, madame, read my letter. It . . . will explain my visit."

In his letter, which began by mentioning his second visit to Meylan, and his letter to her at Vif sixteen years before, he begged her to fear nothing from "the emotions of a heart tutored by the restraint of pitiless reality. . . . I shall know how to control myself," he wrote.

Madame Fornier read the letter and, laying it on the mantle-piece, said: "You have been to Meylan again! No doubt it was a chance visit? You did not make the journey on purpose?"

Here was his cue, but Berlioz kept his promise to control himself. "Can you suppose I was there by chance? No, indeed! I have long wished to see it again," he said.

After a long pause Madame Fornier was first to speak: "You have had a very eventful life, Monsieur Berlioz." And she told him that she had read his biography by Jean Mèry. Berlioz brushed aside the unworthy volume, promising to send her a "true one" that he was writing himself.

"You write very well," Madame Fornier remarked.

Deviating a little from his promise, Berlioz said that in his *Mémoires* he had spoken of his feelings toward her without reserve, but had not mentioned her last name. She said nothing, just as she had kept silent when he asked her if she had ever received the letter he had sent her sixteen years before.

She changed the subject by saying that her life had been very simple and very sad. She had lost two of her children; her husband had died when the children were still little.

Then after another long silence she said: "I am much touched, Monsieur Berlioz, by the feelings you have showed to me, and most grateful."

It was her signal to end their interview, but in his suppressed excitement Berlioz missed the hint. Looking at her with "hungry eyes," as he later recalled, and trying to reconstruct in his imagination her vanished youth and beauty, he begged her to give him her hand.

Madame Fornier gave it to him as simply as she would in bidding someone goodby. Hector carried it to his lips and then asked her if he might occasionally write and visit her. She saw no objection to his request, but she said she was not going to be in Lyons much longer. One of her sons was going to be married and she would live with him in Geneva. "Fare-

well, Monsieur Berlioz," she said, "I am deeply grateful for the feelings you have preserved toward me."

He kissed her hand again and tore himself away.

As if in a dream he walked about the streets of Lyons. By chance, he met the brother-in-law of Adelina Patti, then the most famous singer in the world. She was to sing in *The Barber of Seville* on the following night, and her brother-in-law now offered a box for the performance to Berlioz.

Berlioz was planning to go back to Paris that night, but here, he thought, was an excellent pretext for seeing Madame Fornier once more. He rushed back to her house Her maid told him that she had already left. He left her a message, inviting her to Patti's performance, but saying he would have to have her answer before six in the evening, otherwise he would leave for Paris as he originally planned.

He returned to his hotel, but minutes which to him seemed

Overlooking the Rhone river in Lyons

like hours passed without his hearing from Madame Fornier. He tried to read a book, but did not understand a word he read; he paced up and down the room, threw himself on his bed, and finally went out. Before he realized, he found himself again in front of her house. He rang the bell. There was no answer. Perhaps she had anticipated his return and did not want to see him, Berlioz thought, tormenting himself. He walked the street for another hour and this time when he returned he sent the porter's boy to ring her bell. There was no answer.

He let another hour go by and again went back to the house. As he ascended the stairs he heard and then saw two women coming down toward him speaking German. They were followed by Madame Fornier with a letter in her hand.

"Oh, Monsieur Berlioz, you have come for an answer. I have written you one and was just going to leave it at your hotel. I regret I am unable to accept your kind invitation. I have an engagement in the country with my two friends which I must keep. I am terribly sorry to have kept you waiting with my reply, but I have just returned home." She was going to put the letter into her handbag, but Berlioz begged her to give it to him.

She did not introduce him to her friends. In silence they walked out of the house. "Then I shall not see you again?" Berlioz asked.

"You are leaving tonight? Well, goodby, Monsieur Berlioz, and have a pleasant journey."

This was even more final than when he had parted from her a few hours before, but he missed the obvious insinuation because of his joy at seeing her again, and the "affectionate feelings," with which she closed the note she gave him.

Once on the train and later back in Paris he tortured himself with regrets for not having remained in Lyons. What was the hurry to get back to Paris? he cursed himself. After a few days he could no longer restrain himself from writing her:

"Madame,

"You received me with a simple and dignified kindliness of which few women would have been capable under the circumstances. A thousand blessings on you!

"Nevertheless, I have suffered cruelly since leaving you. In vain I tell myself that nothing could have been kinder than your reception, that any other would have been either unsuitable or inhuman; my wretched heart bleeds as though it had been wounded. I ask myself the reason and this is what it is—it is that I saw too little of you, that I did not say a quarter of what I had to say, and that when I went away it was as though there were to be an eternal separation between us. And yet you gave me your hand—I pressed it to my forehead and my lips, and I restrained my tears, as I had resolved to do. But I feel an imperious, inexorable necessity for seeing you again, a favor I hope you will not refuse me. Don't forget that I have loved you for forty-nine years, that I have loved you since childhood, despite the storms that have devastated my life. The proof of this is the emotion I now feel; if it had ceased to exist, even for a day, it could never have been revived under present circumstances.

"How many women have ever heard such a declaration as this? Don't take me for a fool who is the victim of his imagination. It is simply that I am endowed with a keen sensitivity, combined, believe me, with great depths of insight. But my true affections are intensely powerful, and of unalterable constancy. I have loved you, I still love you, I shall always love you. And yet I am sixty-one years of age. I know the world, and I have no illusions left. Grant me then—not as a sister of mercy ministering unto a sick man, but as a noble-hearted woman healing the sorrows of which she is the unconscious cause—grant me, please, the three things which alone can restore my peace of mind: permission to write you occasionally, an assurance that my letters will be answered, and the promise that you will invite me to visit you at least once a year. My visits might be inopportune, and therefore troublesome, if they were made without your permission, and so I will never go either to Geneva or elsewhere unless you write the word—'Come.'

"Who can find anything unsuitable or odd in this? What can be more pure than such a relationship? Are we not both free? Who could be heartless or senseless enough to blame us? No one, not even your sons, who are, as I know, most distinguished young men. I must, however, confess that it would be dreadful to see you only in the presence of others. If you should bid me come, I must be able to converse with you as I did at our first meeting last Friday—a meeting which I dared not prolong, and the sad charm of which I could not enjoy because of my terrible efforts to restrain my emotions.

"Oh! madame, madame, I have but one aim left in the world—that of obtaining your affection. Let me try to attain it. I will be discreet and reserved; our correspondence shall be only as frequent as you desire. I shall never become a wearisome task to you; a few lines from your hand will suffice. My visits may only be few and far apart, but I shall know that in thought we are no longer apart, and that after many years in which I have meant nothing to you, I have at last the hope of becoming your friend. And a devoted friend such as I shall be is rare. I shall surround you with profound and sweet tenderness, and with complete affection in which the innocent trust of the child will blend with the feelings of the man. Perhaps you will find some charm in it, perhaps you will one day say: 'I am your friend,' and admit that I deserve your friendship.

"Farewell, madame. I have just reread your note, and at the end of it I notice again an assurance of your *affectionate feelings*. This is not a commonplace formality, is it? . . . is it?

"Yours eternally,

"Hector Berlioz

"P.S.—I am sending you three books; perhaps you would look through them in your spare moments. You understand that it is an author's pretext to induce you to think a little of him."

The whole Berlioz episode did not merely surprise Madame Fornier; now, accompanied by his passionate letters, it frightened her. "What answer do you expect me to make to this," she asked her future daughter-in-law to whom she told the entire story and showed Berlioz's letters. Nevertheless, to once and for all clarify her attitude toward the situation Berlioz was so determined to create, Madame Fornier wrote him:

"Monsieur,

"I should feel guilty toward both you and myself if I did not reply at once to your last letter, and to your dream of establishing a relationship between us. I am going to speak from my heart, as candidly as I can.

"I am but an old, a very old woman, six years older than you; my heart is withered by days of anguish from physical and mental distress of all sorts, which have left me without any illusions about the joys of this world. Twenty years have passed since I lost my best friend. I have sought no other; only kept up old relationships and natural family ties. Since the fatal day on which I was left a widow I have said goodby to all pleasures and amusements in order to devote myself entirely to my children and my home. This has been my life for the past twenty years; it has become a habit with me, a pattern which cannot now be broken, for only thus can I find peace for the few days remaining to me on this earth—and everything that troubles their uniformity would be painful and burdensome.

"In your letter you tell me that your only wish is for me to become your friend through an interchange of letters. Do you seriously think that this is possible? I scarcely know you. I saw you for a few minutes last Friday for the first time in forty-nine years. I cannot, therefore, rightly know your tastes, your character, or your qualities, and only this knowledge can form a foundation for friendship. When two individuals have the same manner of feeling and seeing things, there is a possibility of sympathy between them, but when they are separated, correspondence alone cannot establish what you look for in me. For my part, I believe it to be impossible. Besides, I must confess that I am extremely lazy about writing; my mind is as inert as my fingers. I have the greatest difficulty in fulfilling even the most necessary duties in this respect. I could not, therefore, promise to keep up a sustained correspondence with you. I should break my promise too often. So I warn you. If you wish to write me occasionally, I shall receive your letters, but do not look for prompt answers.

"You also wish me sometimes to invite you to visit me. That is no more possible than to say: 'You will find me alone.' On Friday I chanced to be alone when I received you, but when I will be living with my son and his wife in Geneva, if I would be by myself when you come, well and good, but if they happen to be with me at the time, you would have to put up with their presence, for I would be extremely displeased if it were otherwise.

"I have told you my thoughts and feelings with perfect frankness. I think I ought to remind you that there are certain dreams and illusions which should be abandoned when we reach our white-haired years, and the disappointment of all romantic feelings, even of those of friendship, which can have no charm unless they were the result of a relationship established in the happy days of youth. To my mind, it is not the moment for starting a friendship when the weight of years is beginning to be felt, and when those years have taught us how easily it is to be deceived. I confess that I have arrived at that point. My future shortens every day. Why form relationships to be born today and perish tomorrow? Why give occasion to fresh regrets?

"In all that I have just said do not think I have any intention of offending your memory of me. I respect your persistency, and am much touched by it. You are still very young at heart, but with me it is otherwise. I am really old. I am good for nothing else except perhaps keeping a large place in my memory for you. I shall always hear of your future triumphs with pleasure. Farewell, monsieur. Again I sign myself affectionately yours,

"Est. Fornier.

Berlioz in
later years

"P.S.—I received yesterday morning the three volumes you so kindly sent me. A thousand thanks for them."

Berlioz would not have been Hector Berlioz if he had accepted Madame Fornier's letter for what it was—a suggestion to keep his dream to himself and to leave her alone, but said in as kind a way as befits a well-bred lady who has more common sense than her admirer. Berlioz was not merely a Romeo, he was an incorrigible romantic, whose tenacity was one of the main characteristics of his nature, and who never knew when he was defeated. To Berlioz her "very frowns were fairer far, than smiles of other maidens were."

He passed two days and nights scrutinizing every word of

her letter, finding balm for his wounded heart in the few affectionate sentences in her otherwise calm, intelligent, and sober reply.

"Madame," [he wrote her,]

"Your letter is a masterpiece of pensive reasoning. I waited until today [two days] to answer it, in the hope of being able to master the overwhelming emotion it had created in me.

"Yes, you are right. You cannot form new friendships. You must avoid everything that can trouble your existence, etc. But, do believe me, I would not have troubled it, and the friendship which I so humbly asked to have at a more or less distant period in the future would never have become *burdensome* to you. (You will admit that word in your letter must have seemed cruel to me!) I am content that you deign to bestow upon me *some affectionate feeling, a place in your memory, and a little interest in the events of my career.* I thank you, madame. I put myself at your feet. I kiss your hands respectfully.

"You tell me that perhaps, at long and uncertain intervals, I may expect answers to my letters. I thank you again for your promise. What I urge with tears and entreaties is to be allowed to have news of you. You speak with such courage of your years and old age that I dare to imitate you. I hope to die first, so that I may send you a last farewell. If it be otherwise, let me be told that you have left this sad world. Let your son inform me—and forgive me for my request. My letters must not be addressed to mid-air. Give me what you would not deny to any stranger—your address in Geneva.

"I shall not go to see you this month in Lyons; it is plain that you would regard such a visit as an indiscretion. Neither will I go to Geneva for at least a year; the fear of troubling you will restrain me. But your address! Your address! As soon as you know it, send it to me, I beg you. If your silence is meant as a pitiless refusal, a formal prohibition of even the very slightest relationship with you; if you so roughly thrust me aside as though I were dangerous and unworthy, you will be putting the finishing touch to a sorrow which you might so easily have alleviated. Then, madame, may God and your conscience forgive you! I shall remain in the cold darkness into which you have plunged me, suffering, desolate, and devoted to you until death.

"Hector Berlioz"

"What contradictions there are in this letter. How disorderly it is! . . ." Berlioz sighed later, but it was too late—he had already mailed it.

Two weeks of utter misery, known to every lover, passed before Berlioz received Madame Fornier's reply. In the same simple manner she reassured him that she had no intentions of treating him as "dangerous" or "unworthy," and informed him that as soon as she herself knew her address in Geneva she would let him know. It depended on her son, whom she was expecting to return home shortly for his forthcoming marriage.

Again two more weeks passed before Berlioz received the formal announcement of Charles Fornier's marriage. Congratulating his mother, Berlioz closed his short note with: "Yes, life is beautiful, but death would be more beautiful still! To be at your feet, my head in your lap, your hands in mine, and thus to die!" The last sentence was almost a verbatim quotation from his *Lélio*, the words with which he had addressed the then still "unattainable" Harriet Smithson, when she was brought to his concert for the first time.

Still another month passed with no news from Madame Fornier. Fortunately Berlioz was kept busy with the preparations of the second act of his opera *Les Troyens*, which was scheduled for a performance in concert form at the Conserva-

Estelle Duboeuf Fornier

tory on December 18, 1864. Meanwhile, he was pleasantly surprised by a visit from the newlywed Charles and Suzanne Fornier. As much as he tried to restrain himself from speaking about Madame Fornier, he failed to conceal his feelings when her name was mentioned. Besides he soon realized that the young couple were well informed about his courtship.

When alone with Berlioz, Suzanne tried to explain the natural and understandable reticence of her mother-in-law. She told him that his aggressiveness, though flattering to a woman of almost seventy, frightened her, and suggested to Berlioz a more restrained approach. Following her advice he wrote Madame Fornier, for once omitting any reference to his passion for her, and again waited for her reply.

He quietly spent his birthday on December 11 at home and alone, reading congratulatory letters and telegrams from his friends in France and abroad. In Vienna his birthday was celebrated by a performance of his works, including a part of *The Damnation of Faust*, but in Paris he had been so harassed by constant demands for cuts in his score by the committee which was organizing the performance of the second act of *Les Troyens*, that he finally canceled the already scheduled production.

Berlioz's now permanent state of depressior was further aggravated by his neuralgia, from which he had been suffering for the past nine years. The nights were agony for him, which he could avoid only by taking some laudanum before going to sleep. Whenever he felt better he visited friends, a German composer and his wife who lived in the neighborhood. He found in them sympathetic listeners to his discussions of music, and when his pain became too acute they would treat him with discreet care by leaving him alone with his thoughts, stretched out on a sofa in front of the fireplace.

Still without a word from Madame Fornier, he wrote her again describing his sad state and complaining about "the lesson" she had given him. "You have driven it home with such cruel force," he wrote her. "I know, men like me are unreasonable. . . . No, I don't wish to give you the slightest annoyance; I will write you only as seldom as possible. You can answer, or not, as you please. I will go to see you once a year, as though merely paying a pleasant visit. You know what I feel, and you will be 'grateful to me for what I conceal.' I fancy you are sad, and that makes me doubly so. . . . But from this day forth I shall restrain myself to a certain way of writing, and on indifferent subjects."

And he closed his letter wishing her "nothing but sweet thoughts, repose of soul, and the happiness she must feel from the assured affection of her sons and friends." "But," he added in the last lines of his letter, "give an occasional thought to poor children who are unreasonable." This time he signed his letter with a formal "Your devoted servant, Hector Berlioz."

Madame Fornier may have been just an ordinary French-woman, to whom great works of art were an unknown vista, who in her common bourgeois life had never been troubled by Shakespeare's dramas, Dante's poetry, or Goethe's fantasy, but she did not lack common sense and a certain sense of humor. In her reply to Berlioz's last sentence in his letter she wrote him: "Believe me, I have some pity for unreasonable children. I have always found that the best way to make them calm and reasonable was to amuse them and give them pictures. I take the liberty of sending you one which will recall to you the reality of the present, and destroy the illusions of the past!" She enclosed a picture of herself.

"An adorable creature!" Berlioz thought as he looked at her gift. But if Madame Fornier had expected the "reality of the present" to "destroy the illusions of the past," she was wrong. She did not know Berlioz. "I can live more peacefully now," he said as he was writing the last pages of his *Mémoires*. "I shall sometimes write to her; she will answer me. I shall go to see her. I know where she is, and I shall never be in ignorance of the changes that might occur in her life; her son has promised to keep me informed. By degrees, despite her dread of new friendships, she may perhaps find her affectionate feelings toward me growing stronger. Already I feel a change for the better in my life. The past is not wholly past. My sky is not without its star, and with misty eyes I watch it beaming upon me from afar. True, she does not love me; why, indeed, should she? But she might have remained in total ignorance of me, and now she knows that I adore her.

"I must try to console myself for not knowing her sooner, as I console myself for not having known Virgil, whom I would have loved so much, or Gluck, or Beethoven, or . . . Shakespeare."

Chapter Fifteen

*A*t a concert in Paris at which his *Romeo and Juliet* was going to be performed, a friend of Berlioz pointed to the large crowd filling the hall and said to him: "Look, they are coming, and still coming . . ."

"Yes, I see them . . . but I, I am already gone," Berlioz replied. "Everything comes to one who waits, but unfortunately at a time when one is no longer good for anything." Still it was better late than never.

Berlioz had sent, so to speak, his final resignation to the musical world, but the musical world refused to accept it. In Austria, Germany, England, and Russia the number of performances of his works was increasing steadily, and even France began to show some true appreciation of the remarkable talent of her native son, and of his contribution to art. In addition to having been made an Officer of the Legion of Honor, he was made a member of the Academy—a still higher honor. This cheered him up but little, for Berlioz seemed to have been predestined to live through one more misfortune.

His son Louis was stricken with yellow fever in Havana and

Louis Berlioz, son of Hector Berlioz

died there on June 5, 1867. He was thirty-three years old. Upon receiving the news Berlioz collapsed and refused to see anyone for days. "It should have been I," he kept repeating. He could not sleep; only the large doses of laudanum brought him temporary relief, but his strength was rapidly diminishing. And yet he braced himself to go on a journey to Grenoble to visit his nieces, recently married.

Once there, not far away from where Madame Fornier was living at the time, he did not miss the opportunity of calling on her. Madame Fornier was also in mourning—she had lost a son, and her grief was further aggravated by new financial problems. Although at that time Berlioz was unable to assist her, he later left her an annuity in his will.

Upon his return to Paris he was besieged with offers for concerts in Austria, Germany, and England. William Steinway, of the piano manufacturing company in New York, was ready to pay him twenty thousand dollars to come to the United States, but after receiving an emphatic "No," he had to be content with a bronze bust of Berlioz. It has remained ever since at Steinway Hall.

However, Berlioz could not resist the incessant coaxing by the Grand Duchess Helene of Russia to come to her country. She offered him fifteen thousand francs and all his expenses paid. He would live at her palace and have a carriage at his disposal, and she gave him a free hand in choosing his own programs for concerts beginning at the end of November, 1867, at the Russian Musical Society in Saint Petersburg.

"If I should die from it, at least I shall know that it was worth it," Berlioz said as he set out on his second visit to Russia. This time he was going there not merely for the financial benefits. He well remembered the enthusiastic acclaim he had received in Russia twenty years before, and nowhere else could he have hoped to have such elation from the performances of his works. Far better than the large doses of laudanum, the old drug—the intoxication of anticipating a performance—now brought Hector Berlioz back to life.

At the six concerts he conducted in Saint Petersburg he gave superb performances of Beethoven symphonies, as well as of the works of Bach, Haydn, and Mozart, and to show the Russians how Gluck's music should really sound, he included the second act of *Orphée* with a chorus of one hundred and fifty singers. "The Duchess has given orders that I am to be obeyed in everything. I don't abuse her authority, but I use it," he told the directors of the Musical Society. "In two weeks we shall give the first act of *Alceste*."

The Russians, who until then knew Gluck only through muddled performances by incompetent conductors, went wild in their acclaim and could hardly be stopped from applauding. But the Duchess was disappointed by Berlioz's offering only a few of his own compositions, and to oblige her he added the *Roman Carnival* Overture and *Symphonie fantastique* to his programs.

His sixty-fourth birthday on December 11 was celebrated with banquets and public tributes in Moscow, where he had come for two additional concerts. An audience of twelve thousand in the largest hall in the city heard his *Romeo and Juliet* and the *Offertory* from his *Requiem*. Berlioz, the orchestra, and the chorus of no less than three hundred singers were repeatedly recalled by the frenzied applause.

"Here they love what is beautiful, they lead a literate and musical existence; they have in their hearts something that makes one forget the snow and the cold." And he added in despair, "Why am I so old and tired?"

After two concerts in Moscow he returned to Saint Petersburg for his final appearance on February 5, 1868. "His performances were excellent, enhanced by his tremendous personality," the composer Nicolai Rimsky-Korsakoff reported later. "His beat was simple and clear, although he complained of being tired and spent most of his leisure time stretched out on his back because of his illness."

"With what joy I will beat the last measures of *Harold in Italy!*" Berlioz said, anticipating the time when he could return to France, and go to Monte Carlo "to lie down among the violets and sleep in the sun." And then, of course, he would visit Madame Fornier, who had written him in Saint Petersburg. But although he did go to Grenoble, he was not well enough to go to see her. He never saw her again.

Seven months later, on March 8, 1869, Berlioz died in his Paris apartment in the arms of his aged mother-in-law, Marie's mother. He was given a stately funeral. A company of the French National Guard stood at attention as trumpets blew for the beginning of the ceremony. At Trinity Church the Pasdeloup Orchestra and the singers from the Opéra performed excerpts from Gluck, Beethoven, and Mozart, and the *Hostias* from his *Requiem*. He was the last of the Berlioz line, which had remained unbroken for three centuries.

"Homage to Berlioz" (*Lithograph by Fantin-Latour*)

BERLIOZ

HAROLD
ROMEO
ET
JULIETTE
LA
DAMNATION DE
FAUST
LES
TROYENS

Hector Berlioz was buried in the family vault next to Harriet and Marie at the Montmartre cemetery and, perhaps, not far from Amélie's grave.

In 1865, a few months after he had first met Madame Fornier in Lyons, Berlioz had published at his own expense twelve hundred copies of his *Mémoires*, and he had immediately sent one of them to her. He had made her as immortal as his own name. But, while thanking him for his gift, Madame Fornier corrected him on an error of memory. In all her life, she said, she had never worn a pair of pink shoes.

But why should that matter? Hector Berlioz was a musician and a romantic, whose works and loves were the products of his fantasy, and he should be allowed this poetic license. In his imagination *his Estelle,* whom he saw for the first time as a twelve-year-old boy, did wear a pair of "pink shoes."

SELECTED DISCOGRAPHY

SELECTED
DISCOGRAPHY*

LA DAMNATION DE FAUST (OP. 24)
  Danco, Poleri, Singher, Munch, Boston Symphony
    (in French)   3–Victor LM–6114

L'ENFANCE DU CHRIST (oratorio, OP. 25)
  Bouvier, Noguéra, Roux, Medus, Giraudeau, Cluytens
    (in French)   2–Vox VUX–2009

HAROLD IN ITALY, FOR VIOLA AND ORCHESTRA (OP. 16)
  Primrose, Munch, Boston Symphony
                            Victor LM–2228   **LSC–2228**

LÉLIO (OP. 146)
  Leibowitz, Paris Symphony Association (in French, German)
                                           Lyrichord 71

NUITS D'ÉTÉ (song cycle, OP. 7)
  Crespin, Ansermet, Orchestre de la Suisse Romande
    (in French)   London 5821   **25821**

OVERTURES

  BEATRICE AND BENEDICT, BENVENUTO CELLINI,
  CORSAIR, ROMAN CARNIVAL

    Munch, Boston Symphony (*Also* Royal Hunt and Storm
      from Les Troyens)   Victor LM–2438   **LSC–2438**

  ROMAN CARNIVAL

    Toscanini, NBC Symphony   Victor LM–1834
    Von Karajan, Philharmonic Orchestra
                                Angel 35613   **S–35613**

* Stereo recordings are listed in boldface.

REQUIEM—GRANDE MESSE DES MORTS (OP. 5)

    Giraudeau, Scherchen, Orchestre Théâtre National de l'Opéra,
    The Chorus of the Radiodiffusion Française (in Latin)
                                 2–*Westminster 2227*   **201**
    Simoneau, Munch, New England Conservatory Chorus,
    Boston Symphony (in Latin)
                             2–*Victor LD–6077*   **LDS–6077**

ROMÉO ET JULIETTE (OP. 17)

    Elias, Tozzi, Valletti, Munch, Boston Symphony,
    New England Conservatory Chorus (in French)
                           2–*Victor LD–6098*   **LDS–6098**
    Swarthout, Garris, Moscona, Toscanini, NBC Symphony,
    Chorus (in French)   2–*Victor LM–7034*

SYMPHONIE FANTASTIQUE (OP. 14)

    Von Karajan, Berlin Philharmonic
                  Deutsche Grammophon 18964   **138964**
    Munch, Boston Symphony
                      Victor LM–2608   **LSC–2608**

SYMPHONIE FUNEBRE ET TRIOMPHALE (OP. 15)

    Dondeyne, Chorale Populaire de Paris, Musique des Gardiens
    de Paris (in French)
                         Westminster 18865   **14066**

TE DEUM (OP. 22)

    Beecham, Royal Philharmonic (in Latin)
                               Columbia ML–4897